Christians in a Crooked World

Though this book is designed for group study, it is also intended for your personal enjoyment and spiritual growth. A leader's guide is available from your local bookstore or from your publisher.

Copyright 1988
Beacon Hill Press of Kansas City
Kansas City, Missouri

Printed in the United States of America

ISBN: 083-411-2035

Stephen M. Miller
Editor

Molly Mitchell
Patti Reynolds
Editorial Assistants

Jack Mottweiler
Chairman
David Keith
Stephen M. Miller
Carl Pierce
Gene Van Note
Lyle Williams
Editorial Committee

Photo and Art Credits
Cover photo: Comstock; cover caricature: Keith Alexander;
inside illustrations: Bron Smith

Contents

Chapter 1

What's Wrong with Money —and Lots of It?

by Leslie Parrott

Background Scripture: Ecclesiastes 5:10—6:2

SOLOMON was one of the most materialistic people of all time.

He had so much wealth he ignored his silver and measured his riches only in gold. He replaced the silver goblets in his palace with gold ones. He even plated the inside of the Temple with gold and supplied gold vessels for the altar. If ever a man knew the satisfactions of wealth, it was Solomon.

Yet many Bible students believe Solomon was the unidentified writer of Ecclesiastes, that woeful pessimist who bemoaned, among other things, the worthlessness of wealth.

"Whoever loves money never has money enough," the writer lamented; "whoever loves wealth is never satisfied with his income" (Ecclesiastes 5:10).

Part of the problem with money is that we never know when enough is enough. That's because wealth becomes relative. The sum of $1 million is a life-changing bankroll for one person, but it is a pretty meager investment wad for a billionaire.

Ernie Pyle, the famous reporter of battles during World War II, once reported as a young writer that a man had inherited a "huge fortune of $15,000." When the editor reprimanded the reporter for using the adjective "huge," Pyle replied, "That's according to who does the inheriting." For the man on the receiving end of the $15,000, it really was a huge sum.

But when the new level of riches is gained, the gainer is never really satisfied. He wants to reach a still higher level. This is why Ecclesiastes says, "As goods increase, so do those who consume them. And what benefit are they to the owner except to feast his eyes on them?" (5:11).

Solomon's wisdom helped him eventually discover that the person who works with his hands is the happiest and best off of all people, including the rich. "The sleep of a laborer is sweet, whether he eats little or much, but the abundance of a rich man permits him no sleep" (v. 12).

Solomon's final irony on the worthlessness of wealth comes with this statement: "Naked a man comes from his mother's womb, and as he comes, so he departs. He takes nothing from his labor that he can carry in his hand" (v. 15). In the words of an old cliché, You can't take it with you.

The Unimportance of Money

There are only two observations I want to make on the subject of money.

FIRST, MONEY IS NOT AS IMPORTANT AS YOU MIGHT THINK.

There are plenty of things money can't buy. When a teacher I know of told his materialistic young student that money could not buy happiness, the young man snapped back, "Maybe money won't buy happiness, but it will buy a car, and then I can drive around and look for it." He can drive all he wants, but he won't find it from behind the wheel of even the sportiest car.

Just as money won't buy happiness, it won't buy self-discipline when you need to overcome bad habits. It won't buy encouragement when you are depressed. It won't buy an honest friend when you've been rejected. It won't buy good health when your energy is spent. And it won't buy peace of mind when you're all torn up inside.

Money will provide for the basic needs of the body. Beyond this, it will supply a greater source of financial security—unless another Great Depression hits, and you happen to have your money tied up in the wrong investments. In our culture, money also gives a person status and even respect. But with this status and recognition come jealousies, criticisms, misunderstandings, and bitterness, all of which are often related directly to finances.

Money is a basic necessity in our culture, but it won't buy everything.

One of the dangers in exaggerating the importance of money is that we can become neurotic. We can get to the place where we make irrational, downright foolish decisions about money matters. We start doing things like spending a dollar for gas to drive to a store across town so that we can save a quarter on a grocery item. Or we quibble over a few cents on a necessity of life and spend $100 on a gadget.

There are at least three neurotic ways we can react to our materialistic age that exaggerates the importance of money.

1. We can act as if we are poor when we're not. If we have a dollar, we keep it carefully hidden. Our standard response to giving and living is "We can't afford it." Even when we have adequate financial resources, we act like we don't.

I know plenty of preachers like this. (I use preachers as an illustration because I am one.) Preachers have a reputation for being poor. In fact, they even have cars named after them. I learned recently that among the jargon used by auto salespeople is the term "preacher's car." It's a stripped-down, bottom-of-the-line Ford or Chevrolet.

Reinforcing the reputation of the "poor preacher" are the memories many of us have about days when the salaries of preachers used to be so low that the ministers got special discounts at stores and were food-pounded regularly. Sometimes a church member would even buy the pastor a new suit.

But for the most part, pastors today aren't nearly as poor as pastors used to be. Salaries are beginning to close in with salaries of others who have similar training and experience. And society has recognized this fact. Gone the way of the auto running board is the ministerial discount. Food poundings still happen, but usually only when a new minister comes to town. And thanks to adequate salaries, or Bank Americard, or both, preachers can buy their own suits.

Even so, some preachers who have enough to live comfortably—and laymen, too—send out the distress signals 0.

2. A second neurotic option is to go overboard with self-denial. This is particularly popular among the younger people. They have reacted to materialism with a reckless disregard for their own needs, citing Mother Teresa as their model. I admire this idealism, but I pray the ultimate consequences will not be frustration and disillusionment. To say the least, this kind of poverty reaction to materialism is extreme.

3. A third neurotic reaction, one that is exceedingly popular today, is to start believing all the hype

of the advertisers and to begin spending more than we can afford. Such people tend to drive cars that are bigger and newer than they need. They eat in restaurants they can't afford and buy extravagant knickknacks they don't need; and even when they are financially hurting, they refuse to admit it because they are so committed to the "good life." These people enjoy slogans like "Think rich" or "Tithe on the money you'd like to make."

I know of one Christian, a sincere believer, who is caught up in today's prosperity theology movement. He told a friend that he had just won a spiritual battle over whether or not to get gas at the self-service pumps or the full-service ones. Though he worked for a Christian charity and earned a meager wage, he said he finally decided to go to the full-service pumps.

"I'm a child of the King," he explained. "I need to act like it."

He had actually felt guilty about getting self-service gas. He had felt as though he was dishonoring God by not trusting the Lord to provide the money it took to live like a child of the King.

Today, when this man flies, he goes first class. But he sits on a wallet that belongs in coach. And he trusts in a theology that belongs under a bus.

Of these three responses to materialism, none is appropriate. They are all reactions that go too far to one extreme or the other.

The Importance of Money

There is a second idea I would like to suggest about money.

MONEY IS MORE IMPORTANT THAN YOU MIGHT THINK. Since money cannot go with you beyond the grave, it is important what you do with it here.

Methodist church founder John Wesley did not leave "holiness unto the Lord" as just a slogan on the wall. To him holiness was not only theology, it was a way of life. And as far as Wesley was concerned, nothing more clearly portrayed the Christian way of life than did the manner in which believers used their money.

In his sermon "The Use of Money," he presented three guidelines concerning a Christian and his money. Wesley must have believed the guidelines, for he preached this sermon at least 22 times and then had it printed and distributed widely. Here are the three points he made.

1. **A Christian should make all the money he can.** Wesley believed every job was a calling, just as the ministry is a calling. By urging his people to clean living and hard work, he sent them along the way toward lifting themselves by their bootstraps out of the lower-level jobs and into positions of management and ownership.

2. **A Christian should save all the money he can.** Wesley set the following four limits of expenditure for Methodists of his day.

First, they were to pay everything they owed to others.

Second, they were to provide for their families wholesome food, plain clothes, and the household necessities of life. They were to be economically able to stand on their own feet.

Third, when they died, they were to leave their children with the capacity to provide for themselves within the standards that had been set for them.

Fourth, they were to put away, from time to time, enough money to carry on the worldly business it would take to provide for the first three items in this list. To save or spend more than this was to give in to the evils of money.

3. **A Christian should give all the money he can.** Wesley said men might call him a liar, a thief, and a hypocrite if he left more than $30.00 in his will. He kept his vow. When he died, he left his furniture, six pounds ($18.00) for his burial, and a few shillings in his pocket. He gave away

30,000 pounds ($90,000) from the sale of the books he wrote. In fact, his annual income from royalties, speaking engagements, and contributions to his ministry has been estimated at $125,000. Each year he gave almost all of this away to help the poor.

It is not enough to make all we can and save all we can, but we need to give all we can. The writer of Ecclesiastes understood this need for giving. In his typical pessimistic way he said, "I have seen a grievous evil under the sun: wealth hoarded to the harm of its owner" (5:13).

The writer of Ecclesiastes closes his discussion on the issue of money by mentioning one more evil.

"I have seen another evil under the sun, and it weighs heavily on men: God gives a man wealth, possessions, and honor, so that he lacks nothing his heart desires, but God does not enable him to enjoy them, and a stranger enjoys them instead. This is meaningless, a grievous evil" (6:1-2).

Since you can't take it with you, be sure you have an adequate will made out for your estate. Following a meal at the home of a Nazarene man and his wife, he showed me a copy of their will. It was a joy to see how he had provided for his family, along with his local church, the Nazarene college in which I serve, and the denomination's world mission efforts.

I doubt if he had ever heard of John Wesley's formula on money, but he told me how he was making all the money he could, and saving all he could, so he could give all he could. And to make sure his estate became his final gift, he had made out an adequate will.

In a nutshell, there are only two things to remember about money. First, it's not as important as you might think, for it can't buy the most important things in life. Second, it's more important than you might think, because the way you use it can make a difference in your world.

Leslie Parrott is president of Olivet Nazarene University, Kankakee, Ill.

Chapter 2

How Can I Succeed at My Job Without Losing My Faith?

by Lloyd John Ogilvie

Background Scripture: 1 Corinthians 10:31;
Ephesians 6:5-9

THE AVERAGE North American spends at least 150,000 hours working during his lifetime. Others who start working early in life, take little time off, and retire later in years, may log in as much as 200,000 hours.

Most of us expend at least a third of our lives working. For some, work is a delight; for others, a drag. Work in our society can become a god, or it can be a way to glorify God.

I want to introduce you to four people who have struggled with the issue of glorifying the Lord in their work. Each has given me permission to tell his story. Their experiences point up the difficulty of being God's person in the competitive, status-oriented, title-worshiping world of work.

Tom

Tom's voice was filled with hurt and anguish when he called me to ask if he and his wife could come over to see Mary Jane and me that evening. He sounded so urgent we canceled other plans and were waiting for this successful executive and his charming wife, June. When they arrived, it was obvious that something terrible had happened. Tom looked like a beaten animal. His whole demeanor was crestfallen. June's eyes were red, tears cutting rivulets in her otherwise impeccable makeup.

They sat down on our living room couch, a picture of deflation and disappointment. Tom's voice cracked as he tried to speak. June put her arm around him, trying to give assurance and comfort.

"Out with it, Tom," I said. "What's happened?"

"Everything I've ever wanted is lost!" he said. "All I've worked for years to accomplish is down the drain. All the hard work, the late nights on the job, the missed days off, the skipped vacations, the sacrifices I've made to get ahead didn't work. You know I was up for promotion to head of my division. Everyone thought I was a shoo-in. Today, the president of the company announced that a man from one of the branches was being brought in to take the job. Everyone at work was shocked. They can't believe it. Nor can I. Ever since I joined the company after college, I have been working my way up to that job. I've earned it and deserve it. I've given them my life, and they bypassed me! How could God let this happen?"

June and Tom were active church members. They had recently come alive in their faith. Both had made a deep commitment to Christ during a renewal conference at church. It had changed their lives. They had found new love in their marriage and were seeking God's guidance in being parents to their two lovely children.

As an executive, Tom was admired, successful, and very ambitious. His devotion to his work had moved him ahead quickly. Everything, even his new faith, was marshaled to assure his goal of being vice president of his division of the company. He had purchased a new home befitting the dignity of his anticipated position. The high monthly mortgage payments were dependent on the salary he expected to earn when his life-goal was achieved.

Now on this day his world had fallen apart. His self-worth had been tied to success on the job. The Lord, he thought, had let him down. He felt so certain the influence and power of that position were what the Lord wanted for him. And of course, he had dedicated himself to becoming the best Christian vice president the company ever had. The trouble was, he hadn't been given the job

Tom spent hours in self-pity, incriminating the values and motives of the company president. Why was he bypassed? Then Tom and June were open to pray to ask for the Lord's help to endure the disappointment. Just before we went down on our knees, Tom said something that made our prayers real: "I guess that job had become my real god. I expected the Lord to pull it off for me."

It took more than that time of prayer for Tom's profound insight to take hold and give him freedom and release. Months, and dozens of conversations later, the realization became the fiber of real conviction. Work, and not the Lord, had been the drummer that beat the driving cadences of his life. To begin to march to a different Drummer was the most painful transition in Tom's life.

Al

Al's story has a different twist. He was driven not just by the need for success, but by fear of failure. He had been raised in a Christian home where hard work, not just cleanliness, was next to godliness. His parents had risen out of the mire of poverty. Industriousness and faith in Christ were syncretized in them both. They had imbued in Al and his four brothers a belief that work and worth were inseparable. Even though his father had suffered a stroke from the strain of overwork, and abhorrence of idleness had made his mother a fretful, anxious person, Al could not shake the impact of their personalities on him.

At work, he was a model of conscientiousness. He took on his own and others' work with gusto. Praise became a narcotic upper to keep him going. Over the years, he slipped into a deadly assumption: What he did on the job made him invaluable. Like Tom, he was a committed Christian. The heady mixture of confusing his production with his worth, and his fear of failing, dominated the attitudes of his life on the job, however. He became more tense as the years rolled by. The more insecure he felt, the more work he took on. Then one day, the creativity and drive burned out. He had become addicted to work. No one worked as hard as he did, he thought. The pity he had gained from his wife and children for how hard he worked didn't satisfy him any longer.

I wish I could give you an "all's well that ends well" conclusion to Al's story. I can't. The most hopeful thing I can report is that Al has accepted the fact of his work addiction and admits that much of the delight of being a father and husband has passed him by. One thing has become clear to him: Until Christ heals his inner insecurity and sets him free to love himself, he will kill himself trying to justify himself by overwork.

Ann

Now I want you to meet Ann. She has risen from her secretarial position to being head of the staff of clerks in her office. Ann is efficient, capable, attractive. She has worked hard over the years to attain high recognition and compensation. Now there is no further advancement open to her.

She can do her job with little thought or effort. Boredom has set in. When she awakes in the morning, the thought of going to work is a drag.

For Ann the real action of life is at church and in her circle of Christian friends. She'd love to resign her job and become a missionary or go to work for the church. There she falsely imagines that every moment would be as adventuresome as the events of the Book of Acts. But the doors seem closed. The most difficult place for her to be a Christian is on the job. "What does running that office have to do with the kingdom of God?" she keeps asking.

Sam

Sam's story is very different. He loves his work. He can't wait to get to the job and is always the last one to leave at night. As a research scientist he's doing exactly what he's dreamed of all his life and prepared for with extensive education, culminating in a Ph.D. with honors. His job is on his mind during every waking moment. And yet, for different reasons, he's ended up in the same condition as both Tom and Al. His problem is that no one is as dedicated to the job as he is. He can't find people to work for him or around him who will give the time and effort to the job he does.

Recently, exhaustion and fatigue have been creeping in. His love of work has become a compulsion. Overburdened, he has become irritable, defensive, cynical, paranoid, and depressed. He's angry at the people whose work he has to assume because of pressures to get the job done on his timing and standards. Stress is evident on his face. His family is showing less excitement and admiration for his hard work. They would like to talk about other things than what he's doing at work. Sam also is a Christian, but he has never thought of his laboratory as a part of his stewardship of all life.

You may have found yourself in the skin of any one of these four people. Perhaps your circumstances are slightly different. But all four press us to ask some crucial questions regardless of where we work.

Here is an inventory that helps to determine whether we are in danger of losing our faith to succeed on the job. I have asked the following questions at conferences and meetings with businessmen and women.

Does work ever compete with the Lord for first place in your life? Do you think about your work a good deal of the time when you're not on the job? Has worry over your work robbed you of peace of mind or interrupted your sleep? Have you ever neglected or misused the essential relationships of life in the family to succeed? Are you ever tempted to compromise what you believe to gain or keep a position?

Is your job one that you can do to the Lord's glory? Has your job and your worth as a person become intertwined? Do you ever overwork as an escape from greater responsibilities? Would you say that you live a balanced, wholesome life of work, recreation, enrichment, and personal growth? Do the people with whom you work know that you are a Christian and sense the influence of your faith in your attitudes, decisions, and values? Have you claimed the place where you work for the Lord and are you a winsome witness and servant to the people with whom you work?

Our answers to these questions directly affect the answer to the basic question with which we began. How can we succeed at our jobs without losing our faith? Allow me to suggest five things that are ingredients of a totally different attitude toward our work.

1. Get a new job! I mean it. Not a different job, but a new one. The great need is to do the same old job differently. That depends on how we look at work.

We take a new job, even in the context of our old one, when we thank God for the privilege of being able to work.

This attitude of gratitude is a sure cure for the drudgery of work. Mark Twain said, "I have always been able to gain my living without doing any work; for the writing of books and magazine material was always play, not work. I enjoyed it; it was merely billiards to me."

That may sound absurd to some of you who groan inwardly when you think about your work. But I think of the writers and speakers I know who approach their opportunities with a grimness, rather than the zest Twain showed. Deadlines are enemies; each line written is a taxing drudgery.

Becoming a new person in an old job is the issue. Can you thank God for your work? Changing jobs will not help if we bring the same attitudes of drudgery to the new one.

And yet, we must honestly acknowledge that many people find themselves in jobs that do not express their capabilities or interests. We need to get to know the real person inside and find work that challenges our aptitudes, experience, and desires. Life is too short to spend it on the wrong job.

2. *Go to work for a new boss!* For the Christian, success on the job is making the Lord the Boss of our lives. We report to the Lord; we serve our employer. Everyone works for some human overseer. Some person is humanly in charge of every realm. Every team must have a captain. Someone bears the lonely task of stopping the buck. The laborer has the job supervisor, the supervisor has the department head, the president has the chairman of the board, and the board members have the investors. Even the self-employed person is dependent on others to utilize his services or assure his investments. We are all intertwined in the fabric of interdependence.

I met an old friend recently. Years ago I'd been with him when he accepted Christ as Lord of his life. As a part of getting reacquainted, I asked a foolish question: "Whom are you working for these days?" I asked this, knowing that his work in the television industry often brought frequent changes of employers. "The Lord!" he responded with a smile. He went on to tell me that the most difficult challenge for him in becoming a vital Christian was to work for the Lord and express that allegiance by doing his best for his employer.

Paul would have been pleased by that. In Ephesians 6:6-7, he gives us the servant's secret of going to work for a new boss. "Don't work hard only when your master is watching and then shirk when he isn't looking; work hard and with gladness all the time, *as though working for Christ,* doing the will of God with all your hearts" (TLB, italics added). There it is: Work for a boss as if working for Christ. That changes both our attitudes and productivity.

In Ephesians 6, Paul goes on to give some stern admonitions to slave owners. His insight packs a wallop for those of us who employ others to work for us today. Insert the words "employer" and "employee" for "slave owners" and "slaves" in verse 9: "And you slave owners must treat your slaves right, just as I have told them to treat you. Don't keep threatening them; remember, you yourselves are slaves to Christ; you have the same Master they do, and he has no favorites" (TLB).

The Christian employer has a major task. When Christ is the employer's Boss, he will do everything possible to clarify goals and expectations, create a healthy working environment, provide affirmation and encouragement, and offer sensitive evaluation and accountability. Caring for employees as if caring for Christ also means concern for personal needs. Praying consistently for the people who work for us changes our perspective from just getting a job done to enabling great people.

3. *Stop working for a living.* Often the question is asked, "What do you do for a living?" The question is ambiguous. For a Christian, Christ is our living. To be independent to preach Christ, Paul earned income by tent-making. His purpose in living was Christ. He did not say, "For me to live is tent-making," but, "For to me, to live is Christ" (Philippians 1:21).

Our god is whatever we think about most of the time. A job can erroneously become a consuming passion. When our work is the essential source of our self-esteem and value system, Christ must take second place.

A friend of mine described a mutual friend who had drifted away from Christ in the pursuit of advancement. "He was born a man, reborn to be a Christian, but died an executive."

But how do we get out of the trenches long enough to find a perspective on our priorities? Years of working with people has convinced me that no one kicks the work habit alone. Like an alcoholic we need other people to help us admit that we are powerless over the narcotic of overwork. That presses us on to the fourth ingredient.

4. Start a new company. Not a new corporation, or a new organization, but a new company of believers with whom you can meet consistently to talk about what it means to live for Christ first and then work with freedom and joy.

I am part of a group that meets for breakfast frequently to talk about the problems of stress on the job. The men in the group come from all walks of life. Many of us are workaholics and need each other to gain and keep perspective. In an unstructured time each person can be accountable to the group and expose ways we drift into making our work our living. We keep tabs on each other's schedules, confess times when our work denies us a full and abundant life. We also talk over mutual problems of pressure we have in common.

The final ingredient of succeeding on the job without losing our faith summarizes all the rest.

5. Bring ultimate meaning to your work rather than seeking to find it in your work. A job should be an expression of the meaning of life we have found in Christ and never a substitute for it. Then we can work with excellence and integrity. We can seek first the kingdom of God and know that He will guide and empower us to bring our responsibilities under His Lordship. Each task or assignment can be done to glorify Him.

In "L'Envoi" Rudyard Kipling describes the future hope of the artist. It envisions what heaven will be for a painter, and yet it contains the essence of what I've tried to say we can live right now on our jobs:

> *When earth's last picture is painted, and*
> *the tubes are twisted and dried,*
> *When the oldest colours have faded, and*
> *the youngest critic has died,*
> *We shall rest, and faith, we shall need it—*
> *lie down for an aeon or two,*
> *Till the Master of all good workmen shall*
> *put us to work anew . . .*
> *And only the Master shall praise us, and*
> *only the Master shall blame;*
> *And no one shall work for money, and no*
> *one shall work for fame.*
> *But each for the joy of working, and each,*
> *in his separate star,*
> *Shall draw the thing as he sees it for the*
> *God of Things as they are!*[1]

Don't wait till heaven for that—start today. Go to work on an old job as a new person. Make the Lord your Boss. Work for Him as your true living. Claim where you work for Him. Make your work meaningful by bringing meaning to your work. Your job is the Lord's as are all the people who work around you. Whatever you do at work—do to the glory of God.

1. From Rudyard Kipling, "L'Envoi," in *Kipling: A Selection of His Stories and Poems,* vol. 2, ed. John Beecroft (Garden City, N.Y.: Doubleday and Co., 1956).

Chapter 3

When I Relax I Feel Guilty

by Tim Hansel

Background Scripture: Matthew 11:28-30

LEISURE has always been difficult for me to incorporate into my life. I have rarely been accused of working too little. My problem has been just the opposite. Overwork is one of the greatest problems for sincere, dedicated Christians today, and I have often been guilty of it. How, then, am I qualified to write a chapter on overwork? The answer is, I am not. Yet that, strangely enough, may prove beneficial because, as you will soon see, I know by experience (a lot of it) the consequences of overwork and busyness.

Play came quite naturally when I was young. In fact, I was accused of overwhelming others with my enthusiasm for play. But something happened. I can remember "growing old" in my early twenties. Work had always been highly esteemed in our family, and hard work was seen as the primary tool for success. I figured if it was good to work 10 hours, it would be even better to work 14.

In college, I seemed to have the energy to withstand the pressure. I remember times at Stanford when I wouldn't even go home at night. Instead, I would push a table up near the door of the cafeteria at 3 A.M. and sleep on it, using my books as a pillow. And then in the morning, when I had to be at work, the first person to open the door would knock me off the table, and I'd wake up and start the day. I convinced myself that I was sleeping "faster" than anyone else.

I had summer jobs that started at five in the morning and lasted until eight at night. I can remember Mom getting up a little after 4 A.M. to fix enormous quantities of eggs and bacon and toast and milk to supply the energy for me to make it through the day. These were special times, important times, and without a doubt, valuable times. But over the years, they did something to my priorities. Work gradually filtered to the top.

During the years when I was a coach and an area director for a youth organization, I would work 12, 14, even 15 hours a day, 6 or 7 days a week. And I would come home feeling that I hadn't worked enough. So I tried to cram even more into my schedule. I spent more time promoting living than I did living. I never knew what Christ meant when He said, "Come to me, all of you who are weary and overburdened, and I will give you rest! Put on my yoke and learn from me. For I am gentle and humble in heart and you will find rest for your souls. For my yoke is easy and my burden is light" (Matthew 11:28-30, Phillips). My life wasn't abundant; it was a frantic sprint from one hour to the next.

I can remember times when fatigue left me feeling isolated and alienated—feelings that previously had been foreigners to me. Unprepared for such parasites on my energy,

I became frustrated, and laughter, which had always been my most treasured companion, had silently slipped away. In 1973, I wrote in my journal:

> When laughter fades
>   the tendency is toward self-absorption
>   and the iris of life's eye
> squeezes the light to a pinpoint.
> Morning only intimidates you into another day
>   and creativity no longer has the energy to care.

In the midst of this season of my life, I received a letter from a girl I'd been dating whom I loved very much (and who a few years later became my wife and mother of my children). In this letter, she included the following quotation from the journals of French novelist André Gide: "Unbearable mental fatigue. Work alone could rest me; gratuitous work, or play . . . I am far from that. Each thought becomes an anxiety in my brain. I am becoming the ugliest of all things: a busy man."

It was a perfect description of what I'd become—the ugliest of all things: a busy man. The words were so painfully true that I *worked* hard to undo their grip on me. And for a short time, I succeeded. The burden of guilt about not working enough was lifted. But deeply ingrained habits don't just disappear. Eventually they surface in other forms. Before long, I was rushing ahead as frenetically as ever.

I was dominated by "shoulds," "ought tos," and "musts." I would awaken unrefreshed in the morning, with a tired kind of resentment, and hurry through the day trying to uncover and meet the demands of others. Days were not lived but endured. I was exhausted trying to be a hope constantly rekindled for others, straining to live up to their images of me. I had worked hard to develop a reputation as one who was concerned, available, and involved—now I was being tyrannized by it. Often I was more at peace in the eyes of others than in my own.

The Western mind and culture leave little time for leisure, prayer, play, and contemplation. Hurry needs answers; answers need categories; categories need labeling and dissecting. The pace I was trying to maintain had no time for rhythm and awe, for mystery and wonder. I barely had time to care adequately for friends and for myself. In order to keep up my incessant activity, God was simply reduced to fit into my schedule. I suffered, because He didn't fit.

Journal entries at this time indicated my readiness:

> I want my life . . . to be more than just work.
> The task now
>   is to live
>   what I was going to say.

It appeared I was at a spiritual intersection. I had to choose between apparent "success," which meant living up to someone else's standards, or true contentment in my own uniqueness, based on a deep and radical kind of self-acceptance imbedded in the unconditional love of Christ. I chose to believe, in more than just words, that what I am is more important than what I do.

As I began to unfetter myself from some of the excessive hurry and overwork, I discovered I was able to enjoy my days and achievements as never before. Before long, my journal entries had a different personality:

> Today
>   one which I've never lived before
>   and one which I will never get to live again.

> Thank You, Lord, for this incredible gift. The surprise of unwrapping it holds wonder and the privilege of excitement.

> By creation . . . I am.

> And that is enough.

Breaking the Spell

How do we break the spell and accept the invitation to a freer life-style? The first step is by letting go of the attitudes that would have us continually deny our health and happiness in an effort to be responsible. Let go of the fears of inconvenience. Let go of the need to constantly compare. Leap out of some of your routines. Begin to refresh yourself in some of the simple joys of being alive.

Some of us need to read the following letter written by an anonymous friar in a monastery in Nebraska late in his life. We probably need not only to read it but also to allow it to seep down into the marrow of our tired and serious bones.

If I had my life to live over again, I'd try to make more mistakes next time.

I would relax, I would limber up, I would be sillier than I have been this trip.

I know of very few things I would take seriously.

I would take more trips. I would be crazier.

I would climb more mountains, swim more rivers, and watch more sunsets.

I would do more walking and looking.

I would eat more ice cream and less beans.

I would have more actual troubles, and fewer imaginary ones.

You see, I'm one of those people who lives life sensibly hour after hour, day after day. Oh, I've had my moments, and if I had to do it over again I'd have more of them.

In fact, I'd try to have nothing else, just moments, one after another, instead of living so many years ahead each day. I've been one of those people who never go anywhere without a thermometer, a hot-water bottle, a gargle, a raincoat, aspirin, and a parachute.

If I had to do it over again I would go places, do things, and travel lighter than I have.

If I had my life to live over I would start barefooted earlier in the spring and stay that way later in the fall.

I would ride on more merry-go-rounds.

I'd pick more daisies.

From *When I Relax I Feel Guilty*, by Tim Hansel, © 1979; used with permission by David C. Cook Publishing Co.

Chapter 4

Warped Work Ethics

by Vern G. Houser

Background Scripture: Isaiah 5:20; Colossians 3:15-17; 1 Thessalonians 5:22-24

SOMETIMES there's no difference between the behavior of the redeemed and the unsaved.
Consider:

- absence for illness without being ill
- misappropriating goods from an employer
- overstating expense accounts
- misrepresenting personal income
- expecting favors based on who we are
- accepting credit that belongs to others
- taking care of personal business on office time

Because there was a lot of stuff that never got written down when they put the Bible together, not all of these ethical issues show up there. Admittedly, some will see references to these in places like the Ten Commandments and the Golden Rule. But not all Christians interpret the Scripture in the same way.

As a result, many complex ethical decisions must be hammered out on the anvil of competing interests. And sometimes this hammering can beat our values into oblivion.

Let's take a look at three church members who spent time at the anvil. They are real people, and the incidents I'll describe really did happen. But I've changed the names and some of the facts to protect the identity of the people.

The Gleaning Field

Ruth is the senior secretary in a public agency. Her personnel file reveals she is an outstanding employee. Her evaluations are filled with praise: pleasant personality, willing worker, arrives on time, works extra hours, is well liked by her peers. Outside the job she has earned the reputation of being an inspiring Christian speaker and workshop leader.

Could anyone find fault with this gracious, energetic, caring woman? As a matter of fact, some coworkers do. To begin with, Ruth's frequent speaking engagements take her away from the office and hinder the work flow. And most of the materials she uses in her workshops are developed on company time, using office supplies.

During a recent discussion on this topic, Ruth explained that she could afford neither the time nor the expense to produce these high-quality materials. Without them her special ministry would become so much chaff. She believes she more than repays the organization with her efforts, so has never questioned the propriety of her actions.

It is Ruth's opinion that the secret of a holy life is a clear conscience, which she says she has. Combine that with the positive feelings resulting from her ministry, and you have the formula for her success. She refers to herself as a 20th-century Ruth and her office as the gleaning field. Indeed, part of her mission consists of diverting secular funds to the sacred ministry. And she sees nothing wrong in this since her church activities help her witness to people on the job. So, in a way, the office gets some eternal dividends on its investment in Ruth and the supplies she conscripts for ministry.

When someone complained that this lady was not doing her share of the office work, her supervisor replied that he was quite satisfied with her effort. Besides, he explained, confronting this temperamental employee would deflate her ego, and she would probably quit. He added that the best guide to an employee's qualifications was a satisfied boss, so the complaint was without merit.

Perhaps the old saying is true after all: God helps those who help themselves.

Some interesting questions surface in this thumbnail sketch of Ruth's office behavior.

1. What standards should guide an employee in the use of time?
2. How should an employee's position or value to the company relate to use of time on the job?
3. What are some implications of trading labor—such as unpaid overtime—for company products or supplies?
4. How dependable is conscience in determining Christian ethics?
5. If winning souls is life's most important mission shouldn't it be carried out at all costs, even if some of the cost has to be passed on to unsaved employers?
6. If everyone lived by Ruth's standards, would we need locks and keys?
7. How should Ruth's supervisor deal with this situation?

Profit or Loss

Jake and his brother are partners in hauling commodities and perishable goods. Smith Brothers Trucking does not enjoy a fine reputation in the business community. The company is known for its meager wages, high profit margins, unsafe working conditions, and poor bookkeeping. Former employees have complained that morale is low, hours are irregular, and equipment dilapidated. Although there is a high level of theft and turnover of personnel, the company resists employee efforts to form a union.

Recently, several of Jake's fellow church members decided to confront him about his business reputation. They found him to be an open, candid person. He began by admitting that the firm was far from perfect. He tried to improve conditions, but his brother's position had prevailed. However, he added that the company had never experienced a shortage of help, and their employees didn't complain to him.

On the other hand, he continued, the workers often took broken cases and odd lots of merchandise home for their own use. It was all part of doing business, with the losses being covered by insurance. Losses resulting from employee theft were just another item appearing in the expenditure column of the company budget.

As a businessman, Jake added, he found it nearly impossible to operate a business and comply with all the petty laws. Nor could he find much guidance in Holy Scripture. The only profit and loss statement in the New Testament was one verse long: "The wages of sin is death, but the gift of God is eternal life" (Romans 6:23). A world full of people in frantic pursuit of survival can't stop to debate the ownership of every coat hanger and candy bar.

Jake justified his business practices by explaining that his every act is based on a good motive. His character, he said, is above reproach, and his family is highly respected in

the community. He has served on various church committees, and commendations and awards from church and civic
organizations decorate the walls of his office.

Jake closed the discussion by saying he took pride that
his church and charitable giving was probably unequaled in
the county. Where the world intersects with the church, he
was God's man standing at the crossroads.

Consider the following ethical issues that are raised in
the account of Smith Brothers Trucking.

1. Is it the obligation of management to use profits to
   improve working conditions?
2. If business losses and employee theft are to be expected, should Jake's lax attitude about this be considered wrong?
3. Are illegal acts always unethical?
4. Should a prospering business be concerned with
   community rumors?
5. Under what conditions should we approach another
   church member about his character or business reputation?
6. Do you agree with Jake that we should just strive for
   pure motives and leave the rest to God?

A Two-edged Sword

Meet Ben, a ministerial student working his way
through college. He works part-time for—guess who—Jake
of Smith Brothers Trucking.

Ben says wages are low, working conditions poor, and
his coworkers worldly. But the weekends are great. They
haul unmarked boxes across the border and upon returning
are paid in cash. No time is kept, and there is no withholding
tax to worry about. A dollar earned is a dollar to spend.

Lately, Ben has been worried that the company might
be allowing illegal activities. He has also noted that the
amount of theft by his peers has been increasing. The young
student has never been involved, but he admits to receiving

some of the spoils as gifts from his buddies. He usually shares the foodstuffs with fellow church members. After all, one family can eat only so much cheese.

Ben has considered reporting his concerns to someone, but he feels the risk is great, and it's likely that nothing would be done about them anyway. And if the guys found out he ratted on them, he would have to find another job. He concluded that this job is only temporary, so he will mind his own business.

In another year he will be in seminary and never again have to grapple with the ethics of the twilight business world. No longer will he be a powerless statistic grouped with the masses. He will form a circle of friends, drop out of this race for survival at any cost, and give himself to reflection and meditation.

The life of today's working student is filled with a maze of options. Consider these questions:

1. Is it a mark of maturity to just accept those things you cannot change?

2. Does the temporary nature of the job excuse acceptance of unethical conditions?

3. What should we do if we are coerced to commit an illegal act on the job?

4. What responsibility does the employee bear for a company's shady business practices?

5. Which is more important, personal ethics or maintaining unity in the group?

6. If we worship a personal God, isn't it His duty to provide guidance in all situations?

7. Will the short-term attitudes expressed here have any long-term effect in Ben's life?

In the conflicts faced by these three Christians, I'd like to be able to give you a precise list of errors they made, as well as corrective actions they need to take. But it's not that simple. In each of these stories, I see only part of the picture. And as I said earlier, sincere Christians often disagree on how to interpret what the Bible has to say about behavior.

But for Ruth, Jake, Ben, and the rest of us, I'd like to raise a caution flag or two.

First, we need to recognize that technology is rapidly changing our society. We are a people who now worship at the shrine of the newest invention. And as technology makes life more impersonal, the traditional ethics that personalize and humanize are too easily discarded. We have moved from face-to-face to phone-to-phone, and now to computer-to-computer. And it's a whole lot easier to rationalize away the cheating of a computer or a large corporation than it is the cheating of a shop owner we know is struggling to feed his family.

Technology isn't the only thing that can distort our ethics. So can today's media. Advertising in particular has keenly developed the science of upsetting the balance of human senses. It can create for us desires we cannot afford or that would eat away at our spiritual foundation, disrupting our relationships with God and with others. And at the point where our self-interest clashes with the good of our fellow humans, we are most prone to allow questionable exceptions.

In every city cathedral, in every wayside chapel, people like Ruth, Jake, and Ben attend church, listen to the sermon, and go away resisting change. The problem is that the liberty one generation assumes becomes license in the following generation's morals.

Our children's theology is formed in the gap that separates our preaching from our practice. Adult indiscretion becomes the springboard from which the youth dive into the deeper pools of self-indulgence and unbelief. We are learning that deviating from the norm because of extenuating circumstances is one thing. It is quite another to see our children deny the norm itself.

We would do well to live with a deep sense of personal responsibility for our thoughts and actions. In foregoing the expedient, we will find clarity of conscience, peace of mind, and a heavenly reward. Otherwise, we will deserve the epitaph written by T. S. Eliot.

> *They were a sensitive, godless people,*
> *Whose only monument was*
> *A thousand miles of asphalt,*
> *And 10,000 lost golf balls.*

Vern G. Houser is assistant superintendent of business services for the Hueneme school district in Port Hueneme, Calif.

Chapter 5

When Does Entertainment Become Sinful?

by Jerry Cohagan

Background Scripture: Ephesians 4:17-24;
5:1-4, 15-17; Colossians 3:15-17

THEY STOOD BACKSTAGE waiting their turn to go on. I just stared at them—four grown men dressed in black and yellow striped body leotards, wearing eye shadow, and growing hair longer than Lady Godiva. They called themselves Stryper.

It was at the 1986 Dove Awards being broadcast live from Nashville, honoring the best in gospel music. And Stryper was scheduled to perform. Now Nashville isn't exactly known for opening its arms to heavy metal rock 'n' roll and new wave music. Couple that with the fact that this particular audience was made up mainly of Christians who had been sitting two hours in gold lamé dresses and rented tuxedos with cummerbunds too tight, people who were more in keeping with the musical stylings of the Bill Gaither Trio, Sandi Patti, and the Cathedral Quartet.

These four human bumblebees took their place on stage during a commercial break, then humbly waited for a sign from the floor director to begin their number. Like me, the audience stared.

When given the sign, they played (very loud), sang (some might say screamed), and moved (some might say danced) to the music of their song, a song proclaiming God's unending love for us and the fact that "by His stripes we are healed" (Isaiah 53:5, NKJV). After the drummer beat his last riff, the lead singer screamed his highest note, and the guitarist pounded his loudest chord, there was only a moment's hesitation before everyone, myself included, rose to their feet and began applauding wildly as these four guys shuffled off the stage.

Why in the world were we showering these fellows with thunderous applause? It certainly wasn't for their subtle musical style or their spandex costumes. In fact, their style of entertainment went against my personal taste in music and I dare say against that of the majority in the audience. Looking back now, I realize what it was we were applauding. We were congratulating four young men who, in a crooked world, had found a unique way to communicate God's love to people who don't normally listen. And in a larger sense we were applauding the freedom of the gospel to use as many methods as it deems fit to convey its message.

This incident reminded me that we believers must constantly guard ourselves from letting our individual tastes in entertainment become spiritual standards we use as measuring sticks for fellow Christians.

There are few things harder to define than entertainment. The same thing that delights one person may irritate another. There exists a totally subjective ingredient. And the challenge is to recognize the difference between a personal bias and a spiritual truth.

Certainly, however, any entertainment we experience, whether it be video, film, print, or music, requires a Christian response. We cannot leave our Christianity in the car as we enter a video rental store or a concert. We have to remember that any form of entertainment is promoting certain ideas, morals, or values that eventually influence the way we think and behave.

Let's Be Selective

As a result, we have a responsibility to select the kind of entertainment that will not point us away from a biblical sense of morality and truth.

Here are the facts. As I write this, one out of every three homes in the United States has a videocassette recorder. In the next couple of years, this will jump to more than one out of two homes. Videos are rented now at convenience stores, shopping malls, and even your local hardware store. In addition to the video craze, there are more magazines, books, and recordings of books than ever before, not to mention albums and cassettes.

As we continue to find ourselves with more leisure time on our hands, we have a responsibility to be accountable for how we use this time.

To make intelligent choices, we must be informed rather than plead ignorance or condemn the entire entertainment industry.

Today, for example, we have more opportunity than ever to be selective in what we view. Reviews often tell us whether a particular film or video is sexually explicit or contains offensive language. Also, the advertising for a film or video often reflects the film's content. How the ads are packaged and what they are appealing to is often a good indication of what the film is like.

Most record stores have demo tapes of every album they offer. You can ask to hear an album before deciding to buy it. We need to be aware of the lyrics and the intent of the music in order to make an informed decision. There are also reviews of films and albums, secular and Christian, in many Christian publications. Also, many Christian bookstores now have video rental departments that offer more wholesome or Christian messages, along with a good selection of Christian music and literature.

With all this information available to us, our measuring stick then becomes not our personal biases but whether the particular entertainment enhances the meaning of life to the Christian or serves only to dull and confuse our sense of biblical truth and Christian ethics.

The Pluses of Entertainment

The positive side of this is that through good entertainment we can experience the emotions of others, identify with their situations, and gain new understanding about ourselves and the human race.

John Gardner, master author and storyteller, says that "true art is moral: it seeks to improve life, not deface it."* He feels strongly that entertainment can be used for the upbuilding of the human spirit; that any artistic medium "is good only when it has a clear, positive, moral effect, presenting valid models for imitation, and eternal verities worth keeping in mind." Although some entertainment may not be viewed as "Christian" in its intent, it can still be uplifting if it points us to Christian truths such as honesty, the beauty of nature, and a sense of justice. And good entertainment examines our humanness with all of its complexities, showing people caught within their life stories and challenged by their choices.

I need to also mention that any entertainment, no matter how excellent, is a hazard if it monopolizes our time. Whenever the majority of our time begins to focus on entertainment rather than on people around us, then it is time to reevaluate our priorities.

All the entertainment styles I've mentioned so far are for spectators. They do not demand audience involvement. I believe we're wise to balance our leisure time by getting involved in entertainment that features some group involvement.

This type of entertainment can strengthen our friendships and our families. My folks love to play table games, and there is hardly a time when I'm visiting them that I do not get roped into a game of Rook, Dutch Blitz, Stock Market, or Uno. The game, in itself, is relatively unimportant to all of us (unless I'm losing). But the game is the medium that gets us all in the same room to talk, laugh, joke, and sometimes yell at each other.

Some of the fondest memories I have of my childhood are the times my family spent together doing things like fishing (where the only thing I managed to catch was my dad's earlobe), putting together a puzzle (I always hid the last piece), or cooking with Mom (did you know vinegar and baking soda don't taste good together?). These times build strong bonds between people.

Of course, it's easier to sit in front of the television, or read a book, or put on the headphones. But if we limit our entertainment to these, I believe we are the losers in the long run. The realness of God in our world must be seen in our relationships with others. And positive, healthy forms of entertainment can help us introduce His reality to a lost and crooked world.

So what about the question at the beginning of this chapter: When does entertainment become sinful?

John Wesley's mother, Susanna, is famous for saying, "Whatever weakens your reason, impairs the tenderness of your conscience, obscures your sense of God, or takes off the relish of spiritual things . . . that thing for you is sin."

I would take license with Susanna's words and say that, "Whatever *strengthens* your reason, *heightens* the tenderness of your conscience, *sharpens* your sense of God, or serves to *enhance* your awareness of spiritual things . . . that thing for you is good." I believe Paul's words to the church at Philippi summarize best what our measuring stick should be when we select our entertainment.

"Finally, brothers, whatever is true, whatever is noble, whatever is right, whatever is pure, whatever is lovely, whatever is admirable—if anything is excellent or praiseworthy—think about such things" (Philippians 4:8).

*John Gardner, *On Moral Fiction* (New York: Harper and Row, 1978).

Jerry Cohagan is a member of the Christian comedy duo Hicks and Cohagan.

Chapter 6

The Gambling Mania

by Carl H. Lundquist

Background Scripture: Matthew 25:14-30;
Luke 12:15; 1 Timothy 6:9-10

WE'RE GAMBLERS, so you'll find us in the casinos about 90 percent of the time," Ellen McGee said to her friends who were celebrating her 70th birthday just before she took off again from Minneapolis for Las Vegas.

Together with a friend, she and her husband make up a trio of high-flying Minnesotans who have an ongoing love affair with the gambling capital of America. During the past six years, the McGees and their friend have flown there 40 times on chartered flights—so many times, in fact, that their travel agency feted them as its most frequent fliers to

Las Vegas. The three of them received gifts of round-trip flights there and were publicized in the agency's magazine. "Actually," said their friend, "we go to Las Vegas an average of once a month."[1] For this trio, gambling has become their regular recreation.

In contrast, in 1983 the sports world was stunned when Art Schlicter, rookie quarterback for the Baltimore Colts football team, confessed to police that he had lost $389,000 betting with Baltimore bookmakers.[2] The former Ohio State All-American was banned from the National Football League as punishment. After a year out of football, he came back, professing that gambling was a thing of the past in his life.

Most adult Americans can be found somewhere between the extremes of fun and compulsion in gambling. An estimated two-thirds of them place some kind of bet regularly. It is a growing problem for the Christian church because its members are being drawn into it innocently, seriously, or compulsively as a result of peer pressure.

A Nation of Gamblers

Our entire nation seems to be on a gambling spree. In one recent year, according to Public Gaming Research of Maryland, legal gambling totaled $24 billion and illegal bets probably exceeded an additional $32 billion. Thus, a total stake of at least $56 billion changed hands through gambling. Consultant and author John Scarne, after conducting a survey of 100,000 gamblers, places the figure much higher—somewhere between $500 billion and $1 trillion![3]

What Is Gambling?

Joan Halliday and Peter Fuller, writing in *The Psychology of Gambling*, defined gambling as "a reallocation of wealth, on the basis of deliberate risk, involving gain to one party and loss to another, usually without the introduction of productive work on either side. The determining process always involves an element of chance and may be only by chance."[4]

Gambling can be distinguished from other forms of risk-taking by three elements that must coexist: (1) a *payment* is involved, for (2) a *prize* to be awarded, on the (3) basis of *chance,* sometimes accompanied by skill.

When any of these three elements is missing, there may be pseudogambling—gaining money without performance or service—but not bona fide gambling. All of life is characterized by risk taking, such as making financial investments, beginning business ventures, or establishing insurance hedges. Yet these risks are different from gambling in that productive work is involved, empirical data is used as a basis for decision making, and adverse experiences often can be offset through wise management.

Why Do People Gamble?

There are several motivations that keep the wheel of chance spinning for Americans. The basic ones:

1. Poverty. So many people live near or below the poverty line that the possibility of making large amounts of money from a small investment is enticing.

2. Greed. People at all financial levels are motivated by greed—the insatiable desire for more. It was called avarice by medieval Christians and listed as one of the seven deadly sins. One 41-year-old store owner, commenting on the 16 years he was on the gambling merry-go-round, said, "I'd close my eyes and see myself winning huge sums of money, hobnobbing with the beautiful people, driving a luxury car. I was the guy who made the casino close the table because I cleaned them out."[5]

3. Entertainment. The legitimate desire for fun and escape leads many to the gambling tables. It is but a small step from playing a game of cards for fun to placing a wager on the outcome. And then it's a somewhat larger step when one joins the professional gamesters to pit his luck—and fortune—against theirs.

4. Excitement. The possibility of winning huge sums and the suspense involved in the action makes the adrenalin flow faster and provides a thrill for the gambler. Many gamblers insist that this is their chief drive.

5. Compulsion. Robert Custer, a Veterans Administration psychiatrist, spoke of compulsive gambling in these terms: "[It] is strikingly similar to a drug habit [and] probably one of the purest forms of psychological addiction known. Compulsive gamblers are stimulated by gambling, get high on it, and have withdrawal symptoms when they stop."[6]

What Options Are There for Gambling?

At this writing, only four states do not permit any legalized gambling. For those who want to gamble legally, at least nine options exist somewhere in the United States:

1. Bingo (legalized in 43 states). While bingo has been stereotyped as a woman's game, it actually is popular with men as well. The stakes are low, averaging $6.00 a night. But in recent years, more has been wagered on bingo than in all Nevada casinos.

2. Horse Racing (legalized in 33 states). Every year in the last three decades more people have paid their way to horse racing tracks than to any of the popular team sports. This is not because they love animals or want to spend an afternoon in the sun. They simply want to make one quick, big killing. And, though 90 percent of all gamblers lose, they hope to beat the odds.

As many as 15 percent of all adults engage in gambling on horses.

3. Lotteries (legalized in 18 states up to 1984 and in additional ones since). About 50 million people buy lottery tickets. Legalized only since 1964, lotteries now outdraw most other forms of legal betting. In one recent year, gamblers spent $1.8 billion on lottery tickets. Because tickets are cheap, lotteries appeal to millions of poor people, causing them to risk money they can't afford to lose. What's more, the odds are heavily stacked against them.

4. Numbers (legalized in 16 states). Tickets are purchased and winner's numbers are drawn similar to the lottery. The game differs in the way winning combinations of numbers are selected. It is just as exploitive. In New York City alone, an estimated 100,000 people play the numbers daily, operators getting 60 percent of the take.

Twenty-five percent goes to the runners (people who transmit the tickets). An average numbers racket man earns up to $60,000 a year. Nevertheless, because the numbers game is low-cost and easily accessible, two-thirds of inner-city adults take this gambling risk.

5. Dog Racing (legalized in 14 states). Since introduced in South Dakota in 1904, dog racing has grown in popularity. It now involves 4 percent of the gambling population.

6. Jai Alai (legalized in 5 states). Of the five states sponsoring jai alai betting—a game similar to handball but with wicker baskets on the arms—Florida leads. In 1983, 6.5 million people spent $500 million on this form of gambling.

7. Sports (legalized in 4 states). Betting on professional and amateur sports has not been legitimized to the same extent as other forms of gambling. As a result, sports betting consititutes the greatest form of illegal gambling in the U.S.

8. Offtrack Betting (legalized in 4 states). This allows a person to gamble on horses without being at the track.

9. Casinos (legalized in 3 states). Nevada and New Jersey are vying to become the gambling capital of the nation. New Jersey now is in the lead because of the proximity of 16 million potential gamblers to Atlantic City's boardwalk. In Nevada in a recent year, $3.6 billion was tallied, with $169.7 million going for state taxes. Nevada has 67,000 slot machines, many in rest rooms and at departing gates at airports. Some casinos pay airfare, lodging, and food costs of their patrons to have a chance at their money.

More than three-fourths of all Americans favor legalized gambling, and many are lobbying in the states to open additional doors. The major arguments being advanced for legalizing gambling are that it will provide revenue for state treasuries, that gambling can better be controlled, that legalization will reduce criminal exploitation, and that legal games of chance will channel a human impulse too powerful to be eliminated by law. These are all plausible reasons and led even the distinguished director of one of America's Crime Investigating Committees to publicly declare himself in favor of legalizing gambling.

What Is the Social Price of Gambling?

Perhaps the most serious price of social gambling is in terms of human dignity when a person becomes addicted to *compulsive gambling*. This fate has befallen up to 10 million gamblers in the United States, according to an estimate made by the National Council on Compulsive Gambling.[7] This suggests that already there may be as many compulsive gamblers in our nation as there are alcoholics.

It is not surprising, therefore, that a self-help organization exists for them also, Gamblers Anonymous. This group defines compulsive gambling as an "illness, progressive in nature, which can never be cured but can be arrested." Symptoms of this illness include his readiness to take chances habitually, his allowing the game to preclude all other interests, his continuous optimism and inability to learn from defeat, his refusal to stop when winning, his risking of too much, and his anticipation of the pleasure-pain tension during the game.

In terms of human damage, compulsive gambling can be extremely destructive. Dr. Robert Politzer, director of the Johns Hopkins Compulsive Gambling Center, estimates that each compulsive gambler disrupts the lives of 10 to 17 other people, including relatives, coworkers, and creditors. The economic cost also is high. The average compulsive gambler usually bets twice what he makes and costs society approximately $40,000 a year.[8]

Another social price of gambling is to be seen in the *organized crime* that it spawns, a loose federation of the Mafia-type groups in control of 75 percent of all illegal gambling. Many of the nearly 500,000 career criminals in the U.S. are involved in illegal gambling.

Society also pays a price in the *corruption of public officials.* This includes police officers, judges, legislators, and commission members.

Estes Kefauver, at one time chairman of a Congressional Crime Committee, reported that in his investigations he discovered in one city that the original bankroll of a quarter of a million dollars for one illegal operation was made in an armored car in which the sheriff owned an interest. The armored car also picked up the proceeds of the illegal gambling operation every day. The guards on the armored car, as well as the guards at the casino, were furnished by the sheriff. Kefauver also reported that in another city the sheriff's brother was operating an illegal lottery in the jail!

In his book *New Complete Guide to Gambling,* John Scarne writes, "No other form of illegal gambling . . . enjoys such effective police and political protection as illegal bookmaking."[9]

Another serious price of gambling is, again, its *exploitation of the poor.* While people of all income brackets gamble, there is ample evidence that a higher percentage of poor people's income is lost in this way. Out of desperation, they reach for possible help only to be driven deeper into poverty and despair. They are the majority participants in the numbers racket and in state-operated lotteries. The publicity given to astronomical lottery winnings in 1984—$20 million in New York and $40 million in Illinois—mask the odds of 13 million to 1 for winning. A critical article in the July 1983 *Harpers* magazine stated that, statistically, death by lightning is seven times more likely than winning $1 million in a typical game in which 20 million $1.00 tickets are sold.

What Christian Concerns Exist?

For the Christian there are serious theological concerns, because gambling contradicts some basic biblical assumptions. However, not all Christians interpret the Bible the same on these points. Traditionally, the Roman Catholic church has taken a lenient stance toward gambling by incorporating Bingo games into its fund-raising programs.

Official Protestant positions have followed a harder line on gambling. But, to be sure, significant exceptions exist on both sides. In my judgment, gambling violates five fundamental theological concepts, which should cause Christians to seriously question the practice.

1. God's universe is one of order and not chance. Long ago, Archbishop of Canterbury William Temple declared that the glorification of mere chance is a denial of the divine order of nature. An old Methodist declaration on gambling states: "The resort to gambling is a virtual denial of faith in God and an ordered universe, putting in its place an appeal to blind chance, prompted neither by love nor rectitude."[10]

2. Advancement in life is based upon work. From the time the first family was expulsed from the Garden of Eden, to this day, work has been ordained by God for advancement in life. The Old Testament reflects this: "By the sweat of your brow you will eat your food" (Genesis 3:19); as does the New Testament: "If a man will not work, he shall not eat" (2 Thessalonians 3:10).

3. Money is a trust to be handled wisely. This certainly is the clear teaching of Jesus' parable of the talents (Matthew 25:14-30). Money here is viewed as a responsibility for which Christians are accountable. In this broad view, not only a tithe—10 percent—belongs to God, but 100 percent of one's income.

Such a concept leaves no place for careless stewardship or for the deliberate courting of the loss of all. Gambling, then, is the direct opposite of Christian stewardship because it is a waste of both time and treasure, two of a person's most valuable assets.

4. Covetousness is to be avoided. Our Savior's warning, "Watch out! Be on your guard against all kinds of greed" (Luke 12:15) certainly must include gambling. Gambling grows out of greed and fosters covetousness. To this can be added the apostle Paul's sober observation: "For the love of money is a root of all kinds of evil. Some people, eager for money, have wandered from the faith and pierced themselves with many griefs" (1 Timothy 6:10).

One gambling addict confessed in a *U.S. News and World Report* article, "You never really come out ahead in gambling. Even when you win, you still lose because you always want to parlay the money into a bigger win—and then you lose it all." Big gamblers usually die poor. The odds are too great.

5. Neighbors are to be loved unselfishly. We are our brother's keeper. We cannot knowingly inflict on our brother the pain and degradation that accompanies gambling. If I win, he loses, and in the process we both lose.

Gambling manipulates people for personal profit. It is unworthy of the followers of Christ. Virgil Peterson, of the Chicago Crime Commission, observed: "Gambling is always based on a desire to get something for nothing, to take something away from someone else while giving nothing in return."

America is afflicted with a gambling mania. But the times do not call for a new generation of bluenoses—people who try to impose their moral views on others—or professional do-gooders. What is needed are Christians who set a voluntary example of personal self-discipline and thereby help turn the tide against gambling.

1. "Ask McGee About MLT," *Sun Country Magazine,* November—December 1984, 8.

2. Peter Axthelm, "An American in Trouble," *Newsweek,* April 25, 1983, 81.

3. *U.S. News and World Report,* May 30, 1983, 27.

4. Joan Halliday and Peter Fuller, *The Psychology of Gambling* (London: Penguin, 1974), 12.

5. James Mann and Gordon Bock, "The Gambling Rage," *U.S. News and World Report,* May 30, 1983, 31.

6. Scott Morris and Nicolas Charney, "Stop It! Swearing Off Gambling," *Psychology Today,* May 1983, 88.

7. *U.S. News and World Report,* August 15, 1980, 40.

8. John Greene, "The Gambling Trap," *Psychology Today,* September 1982, 51.

9. Mann and Bock, "Gambling Rage," 29.

10. Methodist Declaration, quoted in E. Benson Perkins, *Gambling in English Life* (London: Epworth Press, 1958), 100.

Condensed by permission from *Silent Issues of the Church,* by Carl H. Lundquist. Published by Victor Books and © 1985 SP Publications, Wheaton, Ill.

Chapter 7

What Is Wrong with Social Drinking?

by Carl H. Lundquist

*Background Scripture: Romans 14:20-21;
Ephesians 5:18*

ELIZABETH! What a funny place to wind up together! Who would have thought 40 years ago that we'd meet here?" Movie actor Peter Lawford greeted Elizabeth Taylor in 1983 at the center for drug addiction and alcoholism sponsored by former First Lady Betty Ford in the Eisenhower Medical Center at Rancho Mirage, Calif.

The two hadn't seen each other since they'd worked on the films *The White Cliffs of Dover* and *Little Women*. Now they both were patients trying to overcome chemical addiction.

"I was just drinking too much and got sick of it. Never again! I began to see the direction my life was going and decided then and there to check into Eisenhower. It's the smartest thing I've done in ages. What a wonderful feeling I have now," Peter told her, smiling widely.[1] But Lawford may have been too late. Less than a year later he was dead, at age 61.

Never again! What a forceful expression for our times and for people of all ages. Particularly, I would encourage Christian leaders shaping our new generation of young people to help them avoid the trauma of a detoxification center by saying to liquor, *"Never again!"* if they drink. And for those who do not drink, encourage them to affirm: "I will never *start!*"

When I say "never again" or "never start," I include the whole range of alcoholic beverages: distilled whiskey with its 40-50 percent alcohol content, dessert wine with its 17-20 percent, dinner wine with its 12 percent, and beer with 4 percent—anything with ethyl alcohol (ethanol), which causes intoxication.

What the Bible Says

The Bible sets a precedent for taking a strong stance against alcoholic beverages, although sometimes these Scripture passages are overlooked. For example, Judges 13 tells of Samson's mother before she was to bear a son. An angel came to guide her through her pregnancy so that Samson would grow to be the man God envisioned.

"You are sterile and childless, but you are going to conceive and have a son. Now see to it that you drink no wine or other fermented drink and that you do not eat anything unclean," the angel said to her (Judges 13:3-4). So, during her pregnancy Samson's mother was to say no to the wine of the Old Testament.

Abstinence was a lifelong practice for John the Baptist. An angel said to his mother, "He will be a joy and delight to you, and many will rejoice because of his birth, for he will be great in the sight of the Lord. He is never to take wine or other fermented drink, and he will be filled with the Holy Spirit even from birth" (Luke 1:14-15).

While Samson's mother practiced abstinence during her pregnancy, John's was lifelong abstinence. He shared this vow with other Nazarites whose nonalcoholic way of life was a vital part of their dedication to God.

Total abstinence is universalized by the apostle Paul in Romans 14, the passage devoted to dynamic principles about Christian living, Christian liberty, Christian sensitivity to the conscience of others, and Christian devotion to God.

Paul concludes: "Do not destroy the work of God for the sake of food. All food is clean, but it is wrong for a man to eat anything that causes someone else to stumble. It is better not to eat meat or drink wine or to do anything else that will cause your brother to fall" (Romans 14:20-21). Here he extends the principle of abstinence by teaching that it is desirable never to drink wine or eat food offered to idols if your Christian liberty causes someone else to stumble.

What About Moderation?

As an advocate of total abstinence, I'm usually asked the question, "Doesn't the Bible actually teach moderation in the use of alcohol, not total abstinence?"

I've looked critically at the New Testament on this point, having done my Master of Theology work in New Testament Greek. My dissertation was based upon an intensive study of *oinos,* the Greek word for wine used in Paul's Pastoral Epistles.

The word *oinos* occurs alone only 29 times in the entire New Testament and 5 other times as part of compound words. In the Pastoral Epistles it occurs 5 times. In each instance Paul refers to wine as he counsels Timothy and Titus regarding their leadership roles in the church. These instances make it clear that Paul approved of some use of wine by people in the churches pastored by Timothy and Titus.

He instructs: "If anyone sets his heart on being an overseer [a bishop or pastor], he desires a noble task. Now the overseer must be above reproach, the husband of but one wife, temperate, self-controlled, respectable, hospitable, able to teach, *not given to drunkenness*" (1 Timothy 3:1-3, emphasis added).

Does *oinos* in the New Testament refer to fermented or unfermented wine? This is still a live question for many Christians. But few Greek scholars teach that the wine used in Bible days was unfermented. In my judgment, *oinos* in the New Testament and its parallel words in Hebrew in the Old Testament mean fermented wine. In the New Testament no reference is made to a process to keep wine from fermenting. As soon as grapes were harvested, people pressed out the juice by walking barefoot on them in large, hollowed-out rocks serving as vats; the wine began almost immediately to ferment. So much action was in the fermentation that for 40 days the wine couldn't be put in leather wineskins. Once in wineskins, it could be kept for as long as three years. By then, it was no longer good wine. There was no refrigeration —no place for cooling wine to stop the fermenting process. The very fact that the process couldn't be stopped is an indication the fruit of the vine very quickly became fermented.

The Bible's many warnings about drunkenness certainly are another indication that wine made people drunk. "Be not drunk with wine, wherein is excess; but be filled with the Spirit" (Ephesians 5:18, KJV).

One custom during Bible times is still another indication that the wine was fermented. At festive banquets the governor of the feast monitored wine drinking to keep it from becoming excessive. At the feast of Cana of Galilee, where Jesus performed His first miracle, the governor of the feast noticed right away that the last wine was better than the first.

In light of Paul's counsel about wine, many people understandably conclude that moderation in using alcoholic beverages is the New Testament standard. Since Paul counseled, "Don't drink *too* much wine," and not, "Don't drink wine," then our modern principle should be moderation, this school of thought suggests.

However, as most students of Scripture know, there is a difference between a local ancient custom and a universal principle. One of the great challenges of biblical interpretation is to determine whether a custom is only a local, time-bound practice or if it is meant to be universalized as a principle for all Christians in all times.

For example, Paul taught about the role of women. In 1 Timothy 2:11-12 he says, "A woman should learn in quietness and full submission. I do not permit a woman to teach or to have authority over a man; she must be silent."

Today we do not insist that women be silent in church. This is not the *universal* principle. In Paul's world, a woman who spoke out in public reflected insubordination in the family and often was involved in immoral living. So, in first-century culture, it was more becoming to the brand-new gospel for a woman to be silent in church.

The *universal* principle is not silence but an orderly relationship within family life. However one interprets the universal principle—and there are all kinds of applications —the local principle that women keep silent in church is not applicable to our day. The local practice is not meant to be the universal principle.

The point is what was a local practice in one culture and time is not necessarily appropriate for honoring Christ in another culture and time.

In that first-century water-short culture, irreproachable conduct meant moderate use of the primary beverage—unfortified, natural wine. Because rain occurred only part of the year, the water supply was insufficient. Consequently, water was stored in wells and cisterns. However, the water became dirty, and bacteria and sediment developed. For drinking purposes, the wine was combined with three parts water, greatly reducing its alcoholic content. While this practice was not followed in Old Testament times, it was true throughout the New Testament.

The abundance of vineyards in the wine-growing country made the use of wine natural. But in spite of the fact the wine was diluted, its addictive qualities caused some people to drink immoderately and often become drunk. So Paul reminded Christians to keep their conduct irreproachable before God. That called for restricted use of wine. But the moderate use of such diluted wine in New Testament times is altogether different from the moderate use of 20th-century wine.

What then is the principle for today? In my judgment, the universal ideal is irreproachable conduct with regard to alcoholic beverages. I believe that total abstinence carries out this principle more faithfully than moderation in our day.

Four Reasons for Abstinence

Four reasons stand out to me for observing the principle of irreproachable conduct by total abstinence from wine and all other alcoholic beverages, except when prescribed medically:

1. One drink leads to more. Herbert Hills, executive director of Alcohol Problems Association in Seattle, insists that of every three persons who start as social drinkers, one ends as a problem drinker. How can anyone be moderate using a narcotic when its first function is to call for more?

An old Japanese proverb says:

First the man takes a drink,
Then the drink takes a drink,
And then the drink takes the man.

This can begin with beer, lowest in alcoholic content among American beverages. Ansley Cuddingham Moore, a counselor writing in *Christian Century,* noted: "I include beer and wine in my call for abstinence because there are addicts who never touch stronger beverages. A would-be-suicide who never drank anything but beer was recently pulled from a river. Beer had dulled his senses.

"One of my own acquaintances drinks only beer, comes home at night, and when he has consumed a large enough quantity will do violence to his wife. Cases of this kind have driven me as a counselor to oppose the use of beer and wine; they do much harm to people and they are frequently stepping-stones to both whiskey and drugs."[2]

2. One drink encourages others to drink. We never know who can or can't handle alcohol.

In an article titled "Why Teens Drink," published by the National Institute on Alcohol Education and reprinted by the Pittsburgh Press, young people listed five reasons for their social drinking:

a. My parents drink.
b. We had drinking problems in our family, and I got caught up in them.
c. There was an absence of affection in my family.
d. I had feelings of personal inferiority.
e. My friends drink and I felt pressured.

Three of these five reasons for drinking grew out of the drinking habits of others. If you're a Christian seeking to be sensitive to other people, it is helpful to remember that one drink on your part may lead another to begin a practice he can't control. You are your brother's keeper.

3. One drink can lead to deep personal tragedy.
The first glass of an alcoholic beverage could be the first step toward heavy drinking. Personal tragedy may then result, taking the form of physical damage to your body—cirrhosis of the liver, diseased kidneys, increased blood pressure, inflammation of the stomach lining, destruction of blood platelets, and a permanent deposit in the brain known as the THG factor, not unlike that produced by heroin.

Another personal tragedy is alcoholism itself. Ten million alcoholics—which is 10 percent of all American drinkers—have crossed the line and can't control their drinking any longer. They drink alone, they drink often, and they drink profusely; they tend to hide their liquor supply, and their minds often dwell on drinking during the day. They've developed an increased tolerance that allows them to drink even more. But they've become alcoholics. They can't stop drinking.

Besides these 10 million, another 10 million are being treated for the *symptoms* of alcoholism. They are close to the brink but not quite there. Among these number are 1.3 million teenagers who have drinking problems. Five percent of them are already alcoholics. When some mix drugs with alcohol, as many entertainers have done, alcoholism can be fatal. An average of 10 percent of U.S. alcoholics ultimately commit suicide.

A lesser-known tragedy is FAS—Fetal Alcoholic Syndrome. When a pregnant woman takes a drink, she also is giving the liquor to her fetus. That's because alcohol, unlike food, is quickly absorbed into the body's system. Within seconds, 80 percent of the alcohol is in the bloodstream, going to all parts of the body, including the fetus. Fetal Alcoholic Syndrome is the third leading cause of birth defects. Each year 2,000 children are born with physical impairments due to alcohol in their mother's body.

Still another personal tragedy is the befuddled mind. The minimum concentration of alcohol in the bloodstream to indicate drunkenness usually is .10 percent. That danger point is reached quickly. A 6-ounce glass of wine, 12-ounce can of beer, or 1½-ounce cup of 80 proof whiskey are all equivalent in alcoholic content. Three cans of beer will dangerously affect the driving ability of a 160-pound person. Some say one can of beer will affect anyone's ability to drive well.

Carried further, consider the possible effect of alcohol on strategic decision making in government, business, or in military maneuvers.

4. One drink can unlock the door to a Pandora's box of social ills. These include among workers lowered productivity, absenteeism, hangovers, inefficient work, Monday morning blues, and returning home with a headache. All of this costs American industry an estimated $43 billion a year. In a time when America already is losing the productivity race to Japan, Korea, Hong Kong, Taiwan, and even to Mexico, we ought to do everything possible to become more productive—not less.

Accidental death is another social evil in this Pandora's box. Fifty percent of all automobile accidents are due to alcohol consumption by at least one of the drivers. As a result, alcohol-dulled drivers kill 25,000 people every year on our highways. During the Vietnamese War, 57,000 Americans died and our youth protested violently. But during the same period, few raised their voices when 75,000 Americans died in alcohol-related tragedies on our highways and streets.

One person is killed every 23 minutes as a result of drunk driving. A driver who had killed an 11-year-old bicyclist said, "I couldn't see him when I was drunk. But I can see him now. I remember!"

While you know these statistics, you may not be aware that nearly 50 percent of falling, fire, and drowning deaths are also caused by alcohol in the victim.

What's wrong with drinking one glass of wine? One glass can lead to another. One glass can encourage others to drink and go further. One glass will lead many into deep personal tragedy. One glass may open the door to a Pandora's box of social evils.

All of these problems were illustrated vividly by Asa Bushnell in 18 years of downward mobility on the corporate ladder. At age 26, he occupied an influential position as public relations director for New Jersey's attorney general. But nothing seemed as important to him as the next drink. And those next drinks led to a bumpy employment ride—to police reporting, to writing for a weekly paper, to cab driving, to a three-month whirl with the *Phoenix Gazette,* and finally to a ghetto curbside in Los Angeles. "As I sat there sharing an ill-gotten bottle of cheap wine with three newly acquired soul brothers, the question crossed my muddled mind, 'What's an Ivy League college graduate doing in this predicament?'"[3] He had touched bottom. There a friend discovered him and guided him to Alcoholics Anonymous, where he made a remarkable transition back to sobriety and usefulness. But nearly two decades of his life had been wasted.

Against all of this background, it seems to me that it is not correct to say that the New Testament teaches moderation in using alcohol for 20th-century America. The New Testament calls for Christians to be circumspect, to set a good example, to be irreproachable, and to refuse to be squeezed into the world's mold. Such a call establishes a credible base for total abstinence from alcohol, including even a glass of wine.

1. Peter Lawford, quoted in "Peter Lawford Graduates from Drug Abuse Center," *St. Paul Dispatch,* January 23, 1984, 10*a.*

2. Ansley Cuddingham Moore, "The Case Against Drinking," *Christian Century,* November 19, 1952, 1349.

3. Asa Bushnell, "Back from Skid Row," *The Rotarian,* September 1980, 14.

Condensed by permission from *Silent Issues of the Church,* by Carl H. Lundquist. Published by Victor Books, © 1985 SP Publications, Wheaton, Ill.

Chapter 8

Lust: The War Within

Author's Name Withheld

Background Scripture: Matthew 5:8; Romans 7:18-25

I REMEMBER VIVIDLY the night I first experienced real lust. In previous years I had already drooled through *Playboy,* sneaked off to my uncle's room for a heart-thumping first look at hard-core pornography, and done my share of grappling and fumbling with my girlfriend's clothes.

But my first willful commitment to lust occurred during a visit to upstate New York. I was alone, flipping through the city guide of what to do in Rochester, and I kept returning to one haunting photo of an exotic dancer, a former Miss Peach Bowl winner, the ad said. She looked fresh and inviting: the enchanting kind of Southern girl you see on TV commercials for fried chicken—only this one had no clothes on.

Since I was a Christian, I instinctively ruled her show out of bounds for me. But as I settled down to watch an inane TV show, her body kept looming before my mind with the simple question, "Why not?"

I began to think. Indeed, why not? To be an effective Christian, I had to experience all of life, right? Didn't Jesus himself hang around with prostitutes and sinners? I could go simply as an observer, in the world but not of the world. Rationalizations leaped up to support my desires, and within 10 minutes I hopped into the backseat of a taxi headed toward the seamy side of Rochester.

I got the driver to let me off a few blocks away, just for safety's sake, and I kept glancing over my shoulder, expecting to see someone I knew. Or perhaps God would step in, efface my desires, and change my mind about the wisdom of the act. I even asked Him about that, meekly.

No answer.

I walked into the bar between acts and was then faced with the new experience of ordering a drink. Bolstered by my first fiery sips, which I tried to stretch out so as not to have to order another, I sat with my eyes glued to the stage.

Miss Peach Bowl was everything the ad had promised. With a figure worthy of a Wonder Woman costume, she danced superbly and was something of an acrobat. She started fully clothed and teased us with slow removals of each sequined article of clothing. She grinned invitingly. I stared in disbelief. In one final strobe-lit routine she cartwheeled nude across the stage.

The flush of excitement created by my first whiskey, drunk too fast in spite of myself, the eye-popping spectacle of this gorgeous woman baring all and jiggling it in front of me, and the boisterous spirit of the all-male audience combined to overpower me. I walked out of the bar two hours later feeling strangely warmed, intensely excited, and surprised that nothing had actually happened to me. I suppose it's the same feeling that washes in after a big event like marriage or graduation, or the first time one falls in love. In just a few hours you realize that although in one sense everything has changed, in another sense nothing has changed. You are the same person.

Lust shares with sins like envy and pride the distinction of being invisible, slippery, hard to pin down. Was what happened that night a sin? I denied it to myself on the way home. To really rate as lust, I told myself, you must look on a woman so as to desire sexual intercourse with her. Isn't that what Jesus said? Whatever happened that night, I certainly couldn't recall desiring intercourse with Miss Peach Bowl. It was more private and distant than that. What happened, happened quickly, was gone, and left no scars. Or so I thought at the time.

Years have passed since that awakening in wintry Rochester, years spent never far from the presence of lust. The guilt caught up with me, and even that very evening, I was already praying slobbery prayers for forgiveness. For a while that guilt kept me out of live shows and limited my voyeurism to magazines and movies, but only for a while. For years I have fought unremitting guerrilla warfare.

Being the reflective sort, I have often pondered the phenomenon of lust. It is unlike anything else in my experience. Most thrills—scary roller coasters, trips in airplanes, visits to waterfalls—lose a certain edge of excitement once I have experienced them and figured them out. I enjoy them, but after a few experiences they no longer hold such a powerful gravitational attraction.

Sex is utterly different. There is only so much to "figure out." Every person who endures high school biology, or a sex-education class, knows the basic shapes, colors, and sizes of the sexual organs. Anyone who has been to an art museum knows about women's breasts. Anyone who has hauled down a gynecology book in a public library knows about genitalia. Somehow, no amount of knowledge reduces the appeal—the forces may, in fact, work together.

I learned quickly that lust, like physical sex, points in only one direction. You cannot go back to a lower level and stay satisfied. You always want more. A magazine excites, a movie thrills, a live show really makes the blood run. I never got as far as engaging in sex with anyone, but I've experienced enough of lust's unquenchable nature to frighten me for good. Lust does not satisfy; it stirs up. I no longer wonder how deviants can get into child molesting, masochism, and other abnormalities. Although such acts are incomprehensible to me, I remember well that where I ended up was also incomprehensible to me when I started.

The night in Rochester was my first experience with adult lust, but by no means my last. Strip joints are too handy these days. The drugstore down the street sells *Hustler, High Society,* anything you want. I have been to maybe 15 pornographic movies. They scare me, perhaps because it seems so deliberate and volitional to stand in line (always glancing around), to pay out money, and to sit in the dark for an hour or two.

The crowd is unlike any other crowd I mix with—they remind me I don't belong. And the movies, technically, aesthetically, and even erotically, are boring. But still, when a local paper advertises one more *Emmanuelle* sequel, I drool.

I read numerous articles and books on temptation but found little help. All the verbiage and the 10-point lists of practical advice for coping with temptation boiled down to "Just stop doing it." That was easy to say. "How-to" articles proved hopelessly inadequate, as if they said, "Stop being hungry," to a starving man. Intellectually I might agree with their advice, but my glands would still secrete. What insight can change glands?

During those years I prayed to God hundreds of times for deliverance, but with no response. I began to view sex as another of God's mistakes, like tornadoes and earthquakes.

In the final analysis, it only caused misery. Without it, I could conceive of becoming pure and godly and all those other things the Bible exhorted me toward. With sex, any spiritual development seemed hopelessly unattainable.

I have described my downward slide in some detail, not to feed your own interests and certainly not to nourish your own despair if you too are floundering. I tell my struggles because they are real, but also to demonstrate that hope exists, that God is alive, and that He can interrupt the terrible cycle of lust and despair. My primary message is one of hope, although until healing did occur, I had no faith that it ever would.

But healing did begin, eventually with a brief, simple book I picked up one day titled *What I Believe*. It was written by a French Catholic author, François Mauriac. Included in the book was one chapter on purity that stood out from all the other Christian books I'd read on the subject.

After brazenly denying the most common reasons I have heard against succumbing to a life filled with lust, Mauriac concludes that there is only one reason to seek purity. It is the reason Christ proposed in the Beatitudes: "Blessed are the pure in heart, for they will see God" (Matthew 5:8). Purity, says Mauriac, is the condition for a higher love—for a possession superior to all possessions: God himself.

Mauriac goes on to describe how most of our arguments for purity are negative arguments: Be pure, or you will feel guilty, or someday your marriage will fail, or you will be punished. But the Beatitudes clearly indicate a positive argument that fits neatly with the Bible's pattern in describing sins. Sins are not a list of petty irritations drawn up for the sake of a jealous God. They are, rather, a description of things that hinder our spiritual growth. We are the ones who suffer if we sin, by forfeiting the development of character and Christlikeness that would have resulted if we had not sinned.

The thought hit me like a bell rung in a dark, silent hall. So far, none of the scary, negative arguments against lust had succeeded in keeping me from it. Fear and guilt simply did not change my habits; they only added self-hatred to my problems. But here was a description of what I was missing by continuing to harbor lust: I was limiting my own intimacy with God. The love He offers is so transcendent and possessing that it requires our faculties to be purified and cleansed before we can possibly contain it.

I cannot tell you why a prayer that has been prayed for years is answered on the 1,000th request when God has met the first 999 with silence. I cannot tell you why I had to endure years of near-possession before being ready for deliverance.

But what I can tell you is that after reading that book, I prayed to God one more time, asking Him not to cure me of my struggle, but instead to simply let me know He was there. And finally, God came through for me. The phrase may sound heretical, but to me, after so many years of failure, it felt as if He had suddenly decided to appear after a long absence. I prayed, hiding nothing, and He heard me.

I wish I could say that after that prayer, I never encountered another problem with lust. My struggles continued, and I slipped and fell several times. But something in me had changed, something that made it possible to say no to lust with much more regularity and certainty. And even more important, I gained a completely new perspective on purity. Purity was much more than a list of steamy situations for me to avoid. It was rather a positive effort to remove all hindrances to my spiritual growth, and to seek God's presence in my life.

Though the temptations continue, I know God is there beside me. And that has made all the difference.

After reading my story, you can probably understand why I resist giving "practical advice" on lust. There are no 10 easy steps to overcome temptation. At times the power of obsession overwhelms all reason or common sense. And yet, throughout my struggle, I did learn some valuable strategies, which I will add in hope of preventing needless scars.

Recognize and name the problem. If it's lust, call it lust. You must admit your condition before it can be treated. Much of my earlier rationalizations were blatant attempts to shirk the name *lust;* I tried to redefine it.

Stop feeding lust. Killing fantasies is like trying not to think of a pink elephant, and there is no magic solution to this problem. But especially in the early stages of lust you can cut off desires through diversion. By not dwelling on the desires when they begin, you can fight against lust's magnetic pull. The farther down the road you travel through books, magazines, films, and personal contacts, the harder it will be to pull yourself away.

Demythologize it. Sexual stimulations promise a lie. That good-looking model in your magazine is not going to bed with you—in fact, photo sessions that create sexy photos are tiresome and mechanical, not at all erotic. Recognize that *Playboy* centerfolds are heavily retouched, and life is far different from what porn portrays it to be.

Confess its real price. I learned the ultimate price just in time, by watching a close friend who went beyond the point of no return and is today as miserable a person as I've ever met. In my case, lust demanded its tribute in the subtle and progressive loss of intimacy with my wife and with God. My own self-respect also gradually deterioriated.

Trace its history. Professional counselors were helpful in pointing out the root cause of my obsession—my sexually repressed childhood. For some people, lust comes from trying to win back the love of a distant parent, or earning vengeance against a disappointing God, or overcoming feelings of physical inadequacy by feeding myths. Friends and sometimes professional counselors can help you identify the cycle of lust by exploring its history with you.

Work on some positive addictions, such as tennis, racquetball, running, or playing the guitar. I've found that even video games preoccupy me for a time, especially when I travel. When I'm tempted to go to a sexually explicit movie, now I seek out a safe, constructive activity to occupy my evening. The obsession fades, at least temporarily.

Obsession arises from legitimate needs; follow them to their authentic source. I need God. I need female friendship. I need to be loved and to love. I need to feel worthwhile, attractive to someone. Those are my real needs, not the 3-minute rush of voyeurism inside a 25-cent booth. Search out healthy relationships and settings where these needs can be met, and the sexually based substitute may lose its grip. A Christian professor, a mature adult in your church, your pastor, a prayer/support group—some or all of these people may help you at the source of your obsession.

Reprinted with permission from *Leadership Journal,* Fall 1982.

Chapter 9

Affair-Proof Your Marriage

by J. Allen Petersen

Background Scripture: 1 Corinthians 13;
1 John 3:16-18

ON A TRIP to Alaska, Evelyn and I were provided a one-week expense-paid vacation in the fabulous Mount McKinley National Park. We were flown into the park by small plane over deep mountain chasms and beautiful lakes and between magnificent peaks. Breathtaking scenery! We transferred to a sight-seeing bus for the five-hour trip back through mountains to the remote Camp Denali with our congenial host, Wally Cole.

Like kids on their first trip to Disneyland, we were all ohs and ahs and eyes. It was a photographer's paradise. Grizzlies, caribou, moose, Dall sheep, rare birds—we saw them all. And the highest peak in North America, Mount McKinley, was spectacular, awesome, majestic, overwhelming!

But on this forever memorable journey there were also many ordinary signs along the road—warning signs: *Beware of Falling Rock. Do Not Leave the Road. Camping at Your Own Risk.* Also helpful signs: *Scenic Rest Stops. Scientific Station. Historical Monuments.*

Marriage is like that—a long and memorable journey. And it becomes more meaningful when you pay close attention to the signs. And more safe—safe from an extramarital affair. First, the warning signs.

Don't Compare the Incomparable

The truth is, there is no standard marriage. Comparisons are like a revolving door that gets you nowhere. You go round and round and then end up in the same place. You only confirm your conviction that you have a second-class marriage or increase your fear that you will fail in a first-class one.

Your marriage is unique, therefore incomparable. You do not compare a Volkswagen with a Cadillac even though both of them are automobiles and both of them can take you where you want to go. Everything about these cars is different even though both of them have the same essential parts and operate on the same basic principle. The personalities and temperaments of the partners, the inherited family characteristics, the opportunities, training, and experience —these all differ widely in each situation. It is easy to imagine that other marriages are much better than yours, but you really do not know the actual state of anyone's marriage. Comparing your marriage with anyone else's can never be valid or positive. The seeds of marriage success are already in your marriage. You must water and fertilize them.

Your partner is unique. You don't need a new partner. Between you, you have the assets for building a great relationship if you are both really committed to working at it. No one else has the same potential you have—the special combination of strengths that God has given you. All the elements for a satisfying marriage are already there if you will use them. You don't need a new job, a new outside lover, a new face-lift. All of this is right within your grasp if each of you gets a new attitude. These riches are within your reach. But you must reach for them and keep on reaching.

You are standing right now on your own gold mine— your own acres of diamonds. Russell Conwell tells the incomparable story.

There once lived an ancient Persian by the name of Ali Hafed. He owned a large farm, orchards, grainfields, gardens. He had many investments and was wealthy and contented. One day he was visited by an ancient Buddhist priest, a wise man of sorts. They sat by the fire, and the priest recounted the detailed history of creation. He concluded by saying diamonds were the most rare and valuable gems created, "congealed drops of sunlight," and if Ali had diamonds, he could get anything he wanted for himself and his family.

Ali Hafed began to dream about diamonds—about how much they were worth. He became a poor man. He had not lost anything, but he was poor because he was disconcerted and discontented because he *feared* he was poor. He said, "I want a mine of diamonds," and he lay awake nights.

One morning he decided to sell his farm and all he had and travel the world in search of diamonds. He collected his money, left his family in the care of a neighbor, and began his search. He traveled Palestine and Europe extensively and found nothing. At last, after his money was all spent and he was in rags, wretchedness, and poverty, he stood on the shore at Barcelona, Spain. A great tidal wave came rolling in, and the poor, discouraged, suffering, dying man could not resist the awful temptation to cast himself into that incoming tide. He sank, never to rise again.

The man who purchased Ali Hafed's farm led his camel to his garden brook to drink one day. As the camel put its nose into the shallow water, this new owner noticed a curious flash of light from a stone in the white sands of the stream. As he stirred up the sands with his fingers, he found scores of the most beautiful gems: diamonds. This was the discovery of the most magnificent diamond mine in the history of mankind—the Golconda. The largest crown jewel diamonds in the world have come from that mine.[1]

Ali Hafed's diamonds were under his own feet, but he didn't realize it.

Your marriage diamonds are in your own backyard. Don't overlook them. Don't minimize them. Mine them.

Don't Set Your Own Traps

Many affairs are the result of falling into your own self-made and self-baited traps. We naively grease our own slide and unconsciously do the things that set us up for a fall.

Consider first your friends. In a society where flirtation is the norm and an affair is accepted behavior, you must choose and cultivate friends carefully. Friends who treat marital infidelity lightly or tell suggestive jokes or stories are really enemies of your marriage. Avoid them. Since many affairs take place between close friends—couples who have had strong friendships together—loose sex talk breaks down the protective walls, piques the curiosity, and encourages fantasies. The more open and transparent the friendship, the more necessary to keep conversation on a high level. Many a woman has faced the double tragedy of her husband's unfaithfulness with her best friend. Without appearing self-righteous or preachy, you can always find ways to let your friends know that you consider fidelity to be very important. Speak up for marriage—for your marriage.

Another trap we set for ourselves is at the office, on the job. It is no secret that many affairs are spawned in the office and that sexual favors often influence contracts and affect promotions. One attractive and very competent secretary told me how she protected herself. "I turned down all invitations for private luncheons with men in our office —and there were many of them—because I knew myself and I knew it would be difficult not to respond to the admiration of other men. I valued my marriage too much to expose myself to those risks."

You must avoid the magazines and entertainment that lower inhibitions. Take TV "soaps," for instance. It is impossible to build a great marriage and be a devotee of soap operas. Their distorted drama of romance, sexuality, infidelity, affairs, and abortions encourages comparisons, dissatisfaction. Unconsciously you begin wondering why your spouse is not like "John's other wife" or "Mary's secret husband." Such fictional comparisons are bound to result in a feeling that you're being cheated in your present marriage and that an affair would bring release from your boredom. This unrealistic fantasy increases any marriage disappointment you already feel. The disappointed expectations cause you to blame your partner for letting you down. Blaming your partner causes you to become passive in your marriage-building efforts. The result of this decreasing commitment and effort is further marital deterioration. This, then, further feeds the fantasy and sets you up for an affair. It's a vicious cycle. You cannot build a real marriage on a fantasy with imaginary characters.

Margaret Hess, a Detroit pastor's wife, has some practical suggestions for avoiding your own traps.

Draw boundaries in relationships with the opposite sex. A psychologist says he avoids scheduling a woman for his last appointment. A minister keeps a counselee on the other side of a desk and keeps the drapes open. A doctor calls a nurse into the room when he must examine a woman patient. A boss and secretary can avoid going to dinner as a twosome or working evenings alone. A homemaker can avoid tempting situations with neighbors when her husband is out of town. A smart wife won't spend three months at a cottage, leaving her husband to fend for himself. Neither will she look after the husband of some other wife who has gone away for the summer. Nor need a husband show undue solicitude for a wife whose husband must be away on business. She needs to feel a gap that only her husband can fill.[2]

Refuse to Saw the Sawdust

Sawdust cannot be resawn. The past is now history and cannot be relived. You can do nothing about past behavior but learn from it. Refuse to let your marriage today be hurt by what used to be.

Your past can benefit your marriage, or it will blight it. You can learn from it, build on it, and give it to God—or you can park by it, rehearse it, and be seduced by it. The past is a bully who will keep you in fear and render you impotent for the opportunities of your marriage today. Or it becomes a scapegoat so there's always somewhere to place the blame for your unwillingness to change and build your marriage now.

Love keeps no score of suffered wrongs. You throw away the score book and get rid of your weapons of manipulation. Surrender your ace in the hole.

In this way, each day is a new beginning, not just a re-hash of the past. You choose to forgive, to learn from mistakes, and to grow together. As God, upon our confession, buries our sins in the sea of His forgetfulness and never brings them against us again, He then protects us "from behind" (Isaiah 52:12, TLB). Each partner must make a strong commitment to "protect the other from behind," from the self-crippling memories of the past. Remember, yesterday ended last night.

Look Through Your Partner's Glasses

Tom and Jan are special friends of mine in Texas. As we sat around the kitchen table recently, they told me their experience. They had just gone to bed one night. Tom had kind of spread out lying on his back while they were recounting the experiences of the day. With hands behind his head he exclaimed with great satisfaction, "I am supremely happy. We have a great marriage and family, I'm doing well in business, we're in a wonderful church. I don't know how I could be more content."

While he was basking in this euphoria of contentment, he realized Jan was very quiet, then the bed began to shake. Muffled sobs came from the other side of the bed, and Jan broke out weeping. Tom was shocked, then got the surprise of his life when she cried, "How can you say that? I have never been so unhappy and disappointed. Nothing is going right. Everything is a mess." Tom told me, "I couldn't believe it. Couldn't understand it."

Because of the many temperamental and emotional differences of men and women, it is natural that they will judge their marriage differently. One partner may be receiving most of what he wants while the other is disappointed. What may be an ideal arrangement for one is boredom for the other.

Couples often unconsciously feel that to discuss marriage needs openly will create a strain and magnify problems and that it is better to let well enough alone—let sleeping dogs lie. Don't bring the bogeyman into the light. But the opposite is true. While we assume everything is lovely, if we do not know where the fault lines are, an earthquake can be brewing and could blow everything to kingdom come.

Ask your partner now, "How do *you* really feel about our marriage? Where do you see areas of need?" In fact, while writing this chapter at home, I left my study, went to the kitchen, and asked my wife these questions. If she is bored,

I need to know it. If she is hurting, I need to know why. If she feels neglected physically, socially, sexually, I need to know that, or there can be no improvement.

Keep Your Hands Empty, but the Box Full

Marriage is an empty box. There's nothing in it. It is an opportunity to put something in, to do something for marriage. Romance, consideration, generosity aren't in marriage, they are in people, and people put them into the marriage box. When the box gets empty, we become vulnerable for an affair.

If you keep the box full, you can open your hands and release the controlling grip on your partner. Holding your partner often amounts to holding your partner down—keeping your partner controlled. This is done in several ways, for instance, by being bossy, domineering. This kind of husband or wife is usually married to a "weak sister," someone with a poor self-image. A leaner—one who is afraid and will do what he or she is told.

There is a quaint little Pennsylvania Dutch restaurant in a nearby suburb where Evelyn and I like to eat. There's nothing like it in the entire Chicagoland area. The food is superb—unusual variety, deliciously flavored, enticingly prepared, large portions. When we have house guests, this is the first place we think of taking them. And they always rave about it and remember it. There is no fancy decor; in fact, it is quite plain with crowded seating and oilcloth on the tables. No reservations are taken, so we usually have to wait.

Not once have the owners cornered us and made us promise that we would return. Not once have they chained us to the tables to make sure we wouldn't leave them. Not once have they cried and whined, "What will we ever do if you do not come back? Don't you see what you're doing to us? How can we live without you?" Not once have they sent out goon squads to drag customers in. And they have no discount prices.

They just keep their box appetizingly full and their generous hands empty. Every customer is willing to wait patiently for a table and put up with the crowded conditions. He knows he cannot get a better deal anywhere else.

To say it another way, open the cage, but keep the quality birdseed in the feeder.

Activate Love by Your Actions

Though love is the most desired commodity in the world and uncounted volumes have been written extolling and explaining it, yet we still have so little of it and so little understanding of how it works.

It is a sad commentary on our whole society that we are more familiar with the romantic type of love that traffics in mascara, mouthwash, and padded bras. And we continue to exalt it without calling it what it really is—a child's world of wishful thinking. French writer André Maurois put it more crassly when he reflected with disgust, "We owe to the Middle Ages the two worst inventions of humanity—romantic love and gunpowder."

In the words of Katherine Ann Porter, "Love must be learned, and learned again, and again; there is no end to it."

To learn, we must study. And the Bible, by the way, is the only authoritative and completely accurate source book on love to be found anywhere. There are three major passages in the Bible that deal with love, its elements, and its practice.

The Song of Solomon is a detailed and candid story of wedded love. First Corinthians 13 is a chapter showing what love is made of and how it behaves. First John 3 and 4 stress the twin truths that love must first be received from God and then actively given to others. In these two chapters, the verbs *doing, practice, giving, acting, loving* are used repeatedly.

Since love is commanded by God—"Husbands, love your wives" (Ephesians 5:25); "Let us practice loving" (1

John 4:7, TLB)—this shows that love is a choice. God says, "Let us stop just *saying* we love people; let us *really* love them, and *show it* by our *actions*" (1 John 3:18, TLB). Therefore, love is something you do. This takes the mystery and myth out of it, the cheap sentimentality and the irrationality. Love is an art that is learned and a discipline that is practiced. The attention and effort that go into mastering any art, skill, or vocation must be committed to learning to love.

This involves discipline, concentration, patience, and commitment. Since these love actions are a matter of choice, they are not dependent on our feelings. In fact, they may be contrary to our feelings. Just yesterday a wife told me, "I no longer have any feeling for my husband. I cannot touch him, and I don't want him to touch me. And you want me to reach out to him when I feel this way?" Exactly! The repeated positive action can have a positive effect on your feelings.

We do not do what we do because we feel the way we feel. We feel the way we feel because we do what we do. Hypocrisy! you say. "You want me to speak love, express love, demonstrate love when I don't feel like it?" a husband queried. Absolutely. Act "as if." It would be hypocrisy only if your motive were to deceive or manipulate your partner. If your desire is to build a relationship and practice God's truth, God will honor it, and the right feelings will follow.

Newspaper columnist and minister Dr. George Crane tells this enlightening experience. A wife came into his office full of hatred toward her husband and committed to getting a divorce. "I do not only want to get rid of him, I want to get even with him. Before I divorce him, I want to hurt him as much as I can because of what he has done to me." Dr. Crane suggested an ingenious plan. "Go home and think and act as if you really loved your husband. Tell him how much he means to you. Admire all his good qualities; praise him for every decent trait. Go out of your way to be as kind, considerate, and generous as possible. Spare no efforts to give of yourself to him in every way, to please him, to enjoy him. Do everything you can possibly think of to make him believe you love him. After you've convinced him of your undying love and that you cannot live without him, *then* drop the bomb. Tell him how much you hate him and that you're getting a divorce. That will really hurt him."

With revenge in her eyes, she smiled and exclaimed, "Beautiful, beautiful. Will he ever be surprised!"

And she did it, with enthusiasm. Acting "as if." For two months she initiated love actions, kindness, listening, giving, reinforcing, sharing, "doing the very best for the object of one's love."

When she didn't return, Dr. Crane called. "Are you ready now to go through with the divorce?"

"Divorce?" she exclaimed. "Never! I discovered I really do love him." Her actions had changed her feelings. Motion resulted in emotion. The experiment became an experience.

Start Your Own Affair at Home

"Affairs are and will be because people want satisfying, qualitative couple relationships, and if they don't find them in their marriages, they'll look for them elsewhere." That statement comes from Dr. Tom McGinnis, a counseling psychologist in Fair Lawn, N.J.

The most descriptive thing I've read about what necessities a marriage must offer to counterattack the appeal of an affair comes from Dr. McGinnis, mentioned above. It is quoted by Nicki McWhirter of Knight-Ridder News Service.

> Married people seek out or succumb to affairs when they feel devalued and less than fully alive. They are bored. Overburdened. It amounts to being very lonely, and it can happen in a household full of kids and babbling spouse in which there is a backbreaking schedule of "fun" things to do.
>
> People who have affairs have the child's deep longing to be touched, caressed, held, hugged, and kissed, whether they can admit it or not. They want happy surprises. That might mean a sentimental, unexpected gift every once in a while.

More important, it is the dependable gift of time and caring, the present of shared ideas, experiences, stories, nonsense, and games, including sexual games. They want the world to butt out.

They want a loving friend, a pal who isn't judgmental. They want someone to convince them they're still loved, lovable, and very special. For a little while, now and then, they want out from under the grown-up responsibilities that have become predictable, dreary, and difficult.

More than a century ago, Henry David Thoreau said it succinctly. "Simplify, simplify, simplify." Focus on, and stay true to, what is at the center, and like planets around the sun of our marriage, the other elements of life will find their right places. Be faithful, stay faithful, have faith—and happiness will happen.

1. Russell Conwell, *Acres of Diamonds* (New York: Harper and Row, 1915).

2. Margaret Hess, *Moody Monthly,* March 1967, 75-76.

Chapter 10

Abortion:
It's a Matter of Life and Death

by Eric Pement

Background Scripture: Genesis 1:27; Exodus 21:22-25; Psalm 139:13-16

WHICH DO YOU THINK is more valuable—an unborn eagle or an unborn baby?" A pro-life group asks this question and then points to an unusual statistic:

The penalty for killing an unborn eagle in the United States is a fine of up to $5,000, and up to five years in prison. But killing an unborn baby is not considered a crime at all, as long as the mother approves.

About 4,500 unborn children are aborted in this country

every *day*. Most of these are healthy children without any mental or physical disabilities, but are simply viewed as an unwanted burden.

However, the possibility of raising a disabled child is frightening to many parents. So much so that Dr. Francis Crick and Dr. James Watson, who won the Nobel prize for discovering DNA, have recommended that a baby not be declared "fully human" until three days after birth, so that parents might legally destroy it if it appears defective.

Why Take Innocent Life?

Scores of books have been written defending the right to abort, as well as defending the right of the unborn to remain unharmed. I've heard a dozen arguments for eliminating the unborn or defective child, but most of them revolve around two main points:

1. The first is usually called "quality of life." It says, how can life be worth living if you're severely crippled? If a child or an adult is so profoundly retarded that he doesn't even know his own name, the person isn't even as good as an animal. For one family to face the medical expenses of caring for a "human vegetable" or a "basket case" (someone missing all four limbs) is just too much. Also, even if society could afford the high costs, suppose the baby's mother didn't want him or love him? It would be better for all concerned if the child were aborted or dead.

2. The second main point is "freedom of choice." It says the choice to bear a child or to abort should be left up to the mother.

This idea is expressed in a number of ways: "Well, abortion isn't anything for anybody to pass judgment on but me." "A woman should have the right to control her own body and determine her own future." "It's my body, it's my life." "If you don't believe in abortion, you don't have to have one, but don't tell me *I* can't have one."

If you examine these statements carefully, you'll see they are different ways of arguing for freedom of choice. Sometimes these arguments can sound awfully convincing.

Steps on the Ladder of Logic

To judge abortion wisely, we must approach it by examining the fundamentals. In fact, this method should be used when you're trying to understand any difficult subject, not just abortion.

First, consider the basic values, the fundamental issues at stake. What's at the heart of the matter? Question the *principles,* not the program. Next, determine which values or principles should take priority over other values. (One sure way of knowing which principles are more important is by studying what the Bible says.) Look at the exceptions last.

Although exceptions may occur, an exception—a rare, one-in-a-million case—should never force you to toss out a rule that is good 99 percent of the time. Likewise, a fact that is questionable or trivial should never be used to overthrow or "cross out" a fact that is solidly proven and well-established. For example, just because scientists can't figure out how the honeybee is able to fly doesn't make all of aeronautics worthless.

We'll use the step-by-step method in dealing with the sanctity of life. We begin with the foundational question of human beings—why are people important? The answer to this question will set the stage. The next step is to examine the unborn fetus—is it alive, is it human, is it important? Finally, we'll talk about the "hard cases"—when might it be permissible to take away the life of an unborn child?

What Are People Really Worth?

If life came about by a chance accident, and human beings are nothing more than two-legged mobile "computers" using carbon cells instead of silicon chips, then why shouldn't we treat people like machines? Machines have no "rights"—we can chop them up, sell them, or destroy them if they fail to live up to our desires.

However, human beings possess a wholly different character than anything else on earth. Not just because we are alive; plants are alive. Not just because we are social beings; ants and fish are social beings. Not just because we can think; chimpanzees and computers can think.

Humans are unique because we were created by God and bear God's image. From the greatest Einstein to the drunk in the gutter, each person carries a spiritual nature that comes from God—a soul, a character that bears the imprint of the Creator. In Genesis 1:27 we find that God created humankind, both male and female, in His own image.

To most of the world, people's importance depends on whom they know, what they can do, and how much they possess. But in the eyes of God, each person is of enormous importance. God does not value us because of our looks, our strength, our I.Q., or our money; He loves each person individually. Each person is unique and has value, even if that person is "unwanted" by his friends or "unloved" by her mother. Jesus Christ loves that person regardless.

Each person has a right to life, even if he can't "contribute" to society. Jesus identified himself with the outcast, not with the in crowd, when He said, "Whatever you did for one of the *least* of these brothers of mine, you did for me" (Matthew 25:40, italics added). God is no respecter of persons; He does not play favorites.

What Is the Unborn Child?

For some people, the unborn child is just "fetal tissue" or a "product of conception." The implication of such language is that the unborn baby is something less than human.

A few people dislike calling the fetus a "baby" because they don't believe it's alive. Even the U.S. Supreme Court in its famous 1973 abortion decision *(Roe* v. *Wade)* said it couldn't resolve "the difficult question of when human life begins."

However, medical doctors, biology teachers, and even most abortionists admit that life begins at conception. Indeed, 10 years before the Supreme Court's abortion decision, Planned Parenthood distributed a pamphlet that stated clearly, "An abortion kills the life of a baby after it has begun."

This can be seen fairly easily.

The same standards for life used for plants and animals at any level of complexity can be used to show that a fertilized egg or a developing fetus do indeed qualify as "life." The difference between a dead body and a live one is not whether it has DNA or is made up of cells, but whether it carries out certain biological functions. These basic life functions would include consumption of food, metabolism, respiration, elimination of waste, growth and movement, and the capacity to reproduce when the organism reaches maturity. This is how biologists and most dictionaries define "life."

You don't have to be a biochemist to recognize that the embryo carries on all the functions of life from the moment of conception. A simple thing to remember is that if the fetus weren't alive, it wouldn't grow and move.

Is the fetus a human life?

Well, it's certainly not *plant* life! And I don't know too many people who would claim it's a form of bird or reptile life.

On a more serious note, we all know the unborn child is not fully grown, is immature, and so on. But the humanity of an unborn baby can never be doubted, just as the "birdness" of an unborn eagle should never be doubted.

But there's more. Biological evidences for the humanity of the unborn child, however true they may be, still do not convey the whole story.

The Scripture gives the view that can never be seen by biology and medicine. In it, God reveals that He has a plan for each person's life, and that He is involved in our growth and development from the very beginning.

In the Book of Psalms, King David describes his creation by God: "For you created my inmost being; you knit me together in my mother's womb. I praise you because I am fearfully and wonderfully made; your works are wonderful, I know that full well. My frame was not hidden from you when I was made in the secret place. When I was woven together in the depths of the earth, your eyes saw my unformed body. All the days ordained for me were written in your book before one of them came to be" (Psalm 139:13-16).

Seen in this light, the unborn child is not merely a developing human organism (though the baby *is* that, of course). God declares that He has also ordained a purpose and a course of life for that child, standing behind the child's formation in the womb long before it is born.

Now, after looking at the Bible's estimate of human life, and especially the value of unborn children, we can examine the main arguments for abortion in their proper perspective.

When Should Life Be Taken Away?

One final tip on clear thinking: Don't let anyone snow you into thinking that because something is *legal,* then it must be *right.* The two are not the same. It's legal in this country to be a drunk, a pornographer, a racist, and a Satanist. In Nazi Germany, it was once legal to kill Jews. However, just because something is permissible under the national law doesn't mean it's acceptable in the eyes of God.

Now, what about abortion?

If humans are made in God's image and life is a special gift given to us by God, and if unborn children are truly human, then the basic idea of abortion is wrong for the same reason murder is wrong. God gives life to humans, and He forbids the murder of innocent people (see Deuteronomy 27:25). If we have no right to kill people simply because they are ugly, poor, or of the "wrong" color or language, then how can we justify killing people because they inconvenience us financially or do not meet our standards for intelligence?

I have seen severely deformed children, "basket cases" by some people's standards. It is their *humanity* that gives them value, not their marketable skills or their "quality of life." People have value simply because they are human, regardless of what they may be capable of by earthly standards.

But what about freedom of choice?

Certainly we know that men and women have the right to freedom of choice. The United States Declaration of Independence put it this way: that among the rights God has given man are the right to "life, liberty, and the pursuit of happiness." To a certain extent, this right to liberty includes freedom of speech, of religion, of assembly, of occupation, and of things that pertain to a person's future.

However, the right to personal liberty has limits. We cannot shout "Fire!" in a crowded theater, we cannot assemble to overthrow the government, and we may not exercise our rights in a way that endangers or restricts someone else's rights. In short, there is a priority of rights, which is summed up in this maxim: "Your rights end where my nose begins."

One of the arguments for "choice" in having an abortion is that a woman has a right to control her own body. To a certain degree, this is true. However, the unborn child is not part of the woman's body. It has its *own* body, with its own DNA (quite different from the mother's), its own fingerprints (visible at three months), and its own independent heart and bloodstream. Sometimes even the blood type is different! So while a woman may have the right to her own life and liberty, that doesn't give her the right to take away her child's life.

An objection that comes up quite often is, "You may not believe in abortion, but at least give the mother the freedom to decide for herself." But in the case of abortion, what this is asking for is that we give the mother the power to save or kill the unborn baby. Under the normal course of law, we do not give anyone the power to kill innocent people.

Maybe this illustration will help.

In the United States 150 years ago, slavery was acceptable in some states, and the Black slave was not considered a true "person." The Southern states argued that each state should be free to choose for itself whether to permit slavery. They told the North, "If you don't believe in slavery, you can outlaw slavery in your state. But don't impose your values on us."

The United States eventually reached the breaking point on this issue, culminating in the Civil War. Although our national conscience was dim for years on the subject of slavery, it was eventually provoked to see that human rights superseded financial benefit. No doubt the slaveholders supposed that their "majority vote" gave them a right to own slaves. Unfortunately, this interpretation of "choice" took away the life and liberty of millions of human beings.

One of the final problems of the "freedom of choice" argument is that it sees only two possibilities. Either abort, or be stuck with a baby for the rest of your life. This is not true; there are more than two options. The mother could give the baby up for adoption, which would seem to be far more humane than aborting it.

What About the Hard Cases?

Would abortion be acceptable following a case of rape?

As evil and as hateful as rape is, killing the innocent party is not the answer. The baby was not guilty of any crime. The child's conception may have come about through an evil act, but the child itself is not evil and has the same potential for good as any human being. In the rare instance where bearing the baby normally would endanger the health of the mother (sometimes a rape victim is young), special medical treatment to preserve both mother and child should be sought.

A very hard decision must be made when a pregnancy would literally kill the mother. For example, such a case might be an ectopic (or "tubal") pregnancy, or perhaps the discovery of uterine cancer, where an immediate hysterectomy is needed. If the baby continues to grow, both mother and child will die.

On such occasions, where we are faced with two certain deaths (unless God miraculously intervenes), the only alternative is to abort the child. An innocent life is still taken, though we should seek to save the child if at all possible.

The *ideal* solution would be to move the tubally implanted fetus to a safe location within the uterus. Currently, we cannot move the fetus without killing it, but as medical technology advances, this may become possible in the future.

Toward Compassionate Solutions

To sum up, then, a consistent view of abortion is one that begins from the most basic platform—the value of human beings. Then, with compassion we try to work out the best way to solve human problems, while safeguarding human life.

Sometimes two things will come into conflict, such as a woman's right to be free of the cost and burden of pregnancy, and the child's right to live. Obviously, if a wife is unready or unwilling to become a mother, the time to make that decision is before the baby is conceived. She and her husband should take steps to prevent conception.

In the same light, if a woman is unmarried, if she would follow the Bible's instruction to "flee from sexual immorality" (1 Corinthians 6:18) and remain sexually pure, most of the problems of unwanted pregnancy (and most of the reasons for abortion) would be solved. This does not let the men off the hook, though—the problem of abortion is a national sin, and the male's responsibility for this sin is equal to the woman's.

When people have fallen into sexual sin and a child has been conceived in the process, the answer is not to tell the mother to escape the consequences of the sin by killing the child, thus committing a greater sin. The Christian response is to respect the new life that has been created, recognize that it has as much a right to live as any of us do, and do what we can to aid both mother and child in building a new life.

Abortion may never be an easy thing for Christians to talk about. But if we'll remember that we're talking about people's lives and ultimate values, those discussions will become a little less frightening and a little more important.

Chapter 11

A Christian Homosexual I Know

by S. A. Baldwin

Background Scripture: Romans 1:26-27; 1 Corinthians 6:9-11

EVERYONE ON CAMPUS liked Tom. His warm and vibrant personality and his striking physical features won him many friends. A charm about him set everyone in his company at ease. Even on a more personal level, Tom demonstrated leadership abilities that attracted many who lived in the college residence hall.

I counted rooming with Tom an honor. Our relationship grew increasingly close as the school year progressed. Though he hadn't committed himself totally to the Lord, we prayed together often. Many evenings we stayed up late talking about his spiritual questions. The Lord blessed our relationship.

During one of those heart-to-heart talks, Tom shared a personal problem. He was a practicing homosexual. I responded outwardly with loving affirmation, but inside I was repelled.

The following days found me in a stupor. I'm rooming with a practicing homosexual, I thought.

I remembered past situations with Tom and felt angry with him for deceiving me. What sort of game had he been playing before he told me the truth? I felt uncomfortable rooming with him and wondered if it was contagious, though I knew perfectly well it wasn't. My lack of understanding and experience caused me to reel with fear at first. I couldn't help it. Tom—a homosexual? I thought gays walked and talked funny. I had a lot to learn.

Sin or the Sinner?

I knew Scripture resolutely condemns all homosexual activity. Old Testament prohibition of homosexual activity was a part of Israel's moral law (Leviticus 18:22; 20:13). The New Testament, with equal force, condemns homosexual activity (Romans 1:26-27; 1 Corinthians 6:9-10; Jude 7). But rooming with Tom forced me to examine more closely the Scripture's attitude toward homosexuality.

Scripture defines homosexuality only in terms of burning lust and practice. In the Old Testament one finds condemnation only upon those who actually engage in homosexual activity. The idea of a homosexual inclination without the activity itself is never considered.

The same attitude runs through the New Testament as well. Paul writes in 1 Corinthians 6:9-10, "Do you not know that the wicked will not inherit the kingdom of God? Do not be deceived: Neither the sexually immoral nor idolaters nor adulterers nor male prostitutes nor homosexual offenders nor thieves nor the greedy nor drunkards nor slanderers nor swindlers will inherit the kingdom of God." Arndt and Gingrich's *Greek-English Lexicon of the New Testament* translates *arsenokoitēs* as "a male homosexual, pederast, sodomite." This word is a compound meaning "male intercourse." So in biblical times, to be a homosexual was to practice homosexual activity.

All of the offenses Paul mentioned have to do with action, the result of personal choices. Therefore Paul's use of *arsenokoitēs* refers to those who practice homosexuality, not to those who simply have a homosexual inclination. For good reason the *New International Version* translates *arsenokoitēs* "homosexual offenders."

In Romans 1:27, Paul writes of "men committing shameless acts with men" (RSV), and he refers to men who "burned with lust for each other" (TLB). This burning with lust should not be confused with a homosexual inclination. Lust is inextricably linked with volition. Jesus also strongly condemned lust among the heterosexually inclined (Matthew 5:28).

Homosexual lust is not tantamount to a homosexual inclination, just as heterosexual lust is not the same as a heterosexual inclination. The weight of scriptural condemnation lies squarely upon homosexual practice, not on homosexual inclination.

My Change in Attitude

I experienced a change. My study of Scripture and those years with Tom caused me to reexamine my personal attitude toward the homosexual. It wasn't easy to get over my initial feelings of disgust and confusion. But as I listened many nights to him pray and weep over his sexual inclination, I began to weep with him. I often asked God why Tom must struggle so. He did not ask to be a homosexual; he did not want to be one.

Tom also experienced a change. The key for him in dealing with his problem was realizing that Scripture does not condemn those with a homosexual inclination. All of his life Tom had struggled with guilt over his sexuality. He felt scripturally condemned because of a problem over which he had no control. Only when he realized that condemnation came upon his practice, and not his sexual inclination, could Tom have any sense of self-worth.

Tom eventually repented of his activity and prayed for God's grace to help him control homosexual lust. A milestone had been passed at this point in Tom's struggle. He and I could at last pray the same prayer during our prayer time together: "Lord, keep our thoughts pure."

Three months later Tom came to know Christ's sanctifying grace as he totally committed himself to God. But Tom was just as much a homosexual after he made a total commitment as he was before. One thing had changed, though. Tom, by the grace of Christ, had been made holy and pure.

Tom continued to pray that God would miraculously remove this "thorn in the flesh" (2 Corinthians 12:7, KJV). The answer did not come as we expected it to come—no miraculous and instant cures. We soon learned God's ways are better than ours. Tom found a Christian counselor experienced in working with homosexuals. With Tom's dogged resolve to change, and the counselor's expertise, progress was made.

The Healing Begins

I learned many things from Tom. He needed love and acceptance, more than most people. Tom felt rejected by well-meaning but ignorant Christians who demanded he repent of his homosexual inclination. Many in his church refused to fellowship with him, even after his commitment to Christ. Few attempted to understand Tom, to reach out to him with a noncondemning, loving hand. All of this made his emotional healing extremely difficult. But thanks to a loving Heavenly Father who constantly affirmed Tom through sensitive people, he began to grow in Christ. His damaged emotions, which contributed to his homosexual inclination, began to heal.

That person who finds himself with a homosexual inclination needs a touch from the healing hand of Christ. But this healing power must be mediated through our own hands. We must administer the touch of unconditional love and affirmation. Scripture condemns no one for having a homosexual inclination, and neither should we.

Tom and I both graduated from college and went our separate ways. I still hear from him occasionally. He went on to study counseling in graduate school. Tom has made progress in the healing of his emotions. He is happily married and has two beautiful daughters. Still, in his weaker moments, Tom struggles with temptation, but the grace of the Lord has seen him through.

S. A. Baldwin is a philosophy graduate from the University of Kentucky and a free-lance writer.

Chapter 12

How Should We Keep the Sabbath Holy?

by Jan Frye

Background Scripture: Genesis 2:2-3; Mark 2:23-28; Luke 6:1-11

WHILE WALKING past a large furniture store the other day, I read a sign on the front door: "Open, 7 A.M. to 11 P.M., Seven Days a Week."

"Sound like my hours," I muttered.

As a half-time student and a mother of three teenagers, I often devote seven days a week to coordinating people with schedules. But then, I know many people busier than me.

What's wrong with us? Even on Sundays we get up early

to make sure the roast is in the oven before we hurry off to church, just in time to teach Sunday School. Then we grab a choir robe and wedge our way into the line already filing into the sanctuary. After service we say yes to our children's requests to invite friends over for the afternoon. Sunday dinner and cleanup come next. Then my husband and I try to continue our childhood habit of a holy nap. With our eyes partially closed, we hear the teens answer every ring of the phone. Finally one of them knocks softly on the door, not wanting to disturb.

"Yes," I answer.

"Can we drive over to the basketball courts?"

"OK. Just be back by four o'clock for teen group."

"OK. By!"

We hear them tiptoe away and in a few seconds tiptoe back. They knock again, ever so softly.

"Where are the car keys?" the spokesman asks.

"On the kitchen counter."

"OK."

Knock. Knock.

"Sorry to bother you, but *where* on the kitchen counter?"

"Just look," I say, with head raised slightly off pillows.

Knock. Knock.

"We found them," he whispers.

Silence. We snooze awhile, then the alarm clock alerts us that choir and teen group begin in 45 minutes.

A Day for Rest

If Sunday is a day of rest, I'd like to know who's resting. On and on we go. Monday morning leads to Wednesday and then melts into Saturday and back to Sunday again. Sunday certainly breaks the ordinary routine of the workweek, but I sense a need to somehow improve the day—to add sacraments or something. A kind of sorrow passes through me whenever I think of how much I want to fall in line with

God's best intentions for the Sabbath. How can I possibly live out His view for the Sabbath in this day and age? And, what *is* His view?

The Bible says that God himself blessed the seventh day and declared it holy (Genesis 2:2-3), whether we choose to observe the day or not. Just as the gospel remains sacred and true, so one-seventh of our time remains ordained, part of God's best plan for us.

Jews see God's time of rest from creation as crucial to Him, and as much a part of the cosmic order as all His creativity. So they look to God for their example. Clearly, if God needs a day of rest, so do we. No matter what we believe about Sunday or what we do on Sunday, the day exists as an ordered, holy day of rest.

Referring to God's rest after creation, 19th-century Bible commentator Adam Clarke wrote, "He who idles away time on any of the six days is as guilty before God as he who works on the Sabbath when it could be done on the preceding days." But, to me, the meaning of Sabbath rest focuses entirely on what God wants from us and for us on Sunday. I must prayerfully and specifically ask, "What is restful to me?"

A friend of mine says she's sure that a Sabbath nap would frustrate her more than rest her body and mind. She relaxes most by shutting herself in the den and singing along with Christian tapes. Her husband, she says, finds clock making most restful, and her children like swimming. Because of our diverse energy levels and abilities, how can any of us dictate the meaning of rest? With our eyes on Jesus, we must discover as individuals how God wants us to restfully observe Sundays.

Long ago, any Jew who worked on the Sabbath risked punishment by death (Exodus 35:2). But because Jesus said, "The Sabbath was made for man, not man for the Sabbath" (Mark 2:27), we can now live in freedom to bypass strict rules and to tailor-make the most restful Sunday possible.

As God helps us imagine ideas for a wide range of restful Sundays, we will find the day of rest more meaningful.

A Day for Holiness

In addition to resting on Sundays, God instructs us to keep the day holy (Exodus 20:8). Many sincere Christians in previous generations carried out this commission by following a list of dos and don'ts. I remember my pastor-father buying aspirin on Sunday, for instance, only because of a "medical need." He would not consider buying for any other reason. Others felt that Sunday newspaper delivery and reading desecrated the Sabbath, as did eating in a restaurant or participating in sports or recreation.

In short, they believed that sacrificing self-pleasure or convenience on Sunday helped keep the day holy. Of course, in those days nearly every business in town closed on Sundays, in support of the old-timers' honest conceptions of what Sabbath observance should include. Nowadays, however, our culture encourages Sunday sales at the malls, puts marked emphasis on Sunday sport events, and advertises special prices on Sunday brunch.

Is that wrong?

The answers for how to keep Sunday holy lie not in concrete-bound rules concerning restaurant hopping or watching a Dallas-Pittsburgh football game on television. Rather, a responsible Christian must prayerfully search Scripture to discover God's guidelines for a holy-designed Sabbath.

First, the Bible declares innocent those who work to minister on the Sabbath. Jesus himself healed and ministered in other ways on the Sabbath. God sets the Sabbath aside for doing good. He encourages us as clergy and laypeople to minister works of mercy on this day, and this includes helping others both spiritually and physically.

The simplicity of this truth, doing good, encompasses a wide range of choices for all Christians. If God shows me that participating in choir practice is not "doing good" in His sight when compared to how I could be using my gift of faith and praying with someone, then I must honor His Spirit. One Christian may do more good and extend more mercy through choir practice, while another may do more good by using the time to visit a shut-in. One may do good by writing a note of encouragement to a hurting friend or by creating a special listening time for a child.

Depending on one's gifts and interests, nearly all Christians can carry out the limitless possibilities for practicing goodness and mercy. God thought primarily of us when He designed this phase of keeping the day holy.

A Day for Worship

Some of us may occasionally wonder if "getting the family out the door" for Sunday School and church justifies the effort. However, Scripture strongly supports the habit. New Testament Christians celebrated the prime time of the Sabbath by teaching (Mark 6:2; Acts 13:44), sharing in Communion (Acts 20:7), and growing from fellowship with other Christians. What better place can we find to accomplish all this than in church?

I know an elderly Christian woman who suffers with cancer. She lies in bed, day after day, month after month, unable to walk across the room, much less attend church. How can she keep Sunday holy? Ah, when God blessed the Sabbath and offered guidelines to keep the day holy, He thought of Christians in every imaginable circumstance.

The original Jewish Sabbath began at sundown on Friday and continued through sundown Saturday. But after Christ arose from the dead, New Testament Christians purposely began celebrating the Sabbath on Sunday, the first day of the week. In no matter what situation we find ourselves as modern-day Christians, we still can turn our thoughts on Sunday toward celebrating new life in Jesus, another scriptural way to observe the Sabbath (Matthew

28:1, 5-6). The fact that Jesus lives sets Christianity apart from all other religious teachings. What a time and reason to celebrate!

My son says we need to leave our work and cares outside the front door every time we enter the church. Then we sense freedom to focus on Jesus as we worship. And during that time Jesus reminds us of the peace we can have through Him.

The *Beacon Bible Commentary* states, concerning the seventh day: "On this day God's command to man to conquer nature is laid aside and man recognizes a higher law, that he yield himself to God."[1] Ultimately, we cannot faithfully keep the Sabbath restful and holy without yielding ourselves to God. And when we fully yield to God, we can experience a special day, full of being "in the Spirit" (Revelation 1:10).

My heart often aches for a single parent in my church. Within his demanding time constraints, I wonder how he manages to coordinate his work, children, Bible study, prayer, church, plus reach out to others. One day I stopped him in the hallway at church and said, "You know, Phil, I really admire the way you seem to joyfully live for Christ all week and then still overflow with God's Spirit on Sunday."

"Well, if I seem to 'overflow' on Sunday, it's only because that's the day my spiritual battery gets recharged," he said, smiling. "Sunday is special," he added, "because it's like tithing one-seventh of my time. I can count on God blessing my spirit when I look at Sunday as sacred time."

Truly, the Sabbath exists for our benefit. It's a gift of time to refresh our perspective, our bodies, souls, and spirits. As our culture drifts from the general sacredness of time, and specifically from the sacredness of the Lord's Day, Jesus challenges us to live differently—to respect and observe His great plan for a blessed Sabbath.

I respond to Him in prayer with, "Lord, as a Spirit-filled Christian in a hurting world, please teach me to reshape my

Sundays. Show me Your best creative ways to carry out Your Word and experience the Sabbath as You ordained."

1. George Herbert Livingston, BBC, 10 vols. (Kansas City: Beacon Hill Press of Kansas City, 1964-69), 1:37.

Jan Frye is a free-lance writer, active in family ministries of Denver First Church of the Nazarene.

Chapter 13

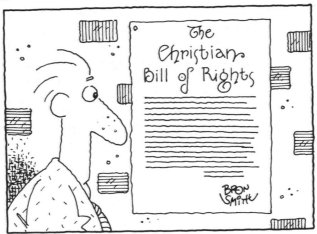

The Christian Bill of Rights

What Rights Do Christians Have?

by Al Truesdale

Background Scripture: Matthew 5:38-42;
Romans 12:14-21; 1 Corinthians 6:1-8

Introduction

MELINDA[1] is 27 years old and the mother of two young children. She has been a Christian four years. She has a problem: sexual abuse: She is repeatedly raped by her husband who is not a Christian and who scorns her faith in Christ.

Melinda lives in Kansas, a state that has a law to protect women against spousal rape. If convicted, a husband can be sentenced as would any other rapist. A friend of Melinda's told her about her legal rights as a citizen. Melinda is desperate and almost ready to take civil action against her husband.

But she has a problem. She believes that if she files charges against her husband, she can no longer be a Christian. She has been told that for Christ's sake Christians willingly forfeit all types of self-defense, whether physical or legal. After all, Jesus renounced it, and in the Sermon on the Mount He commanded His disciples to suffer injustice patiently.

Melinda has read the words of Jesus, "Do not resist one who is evil. But if any one strikes you on the right cheek, turn to him the other also" (Matthew 5:39, RSV). This appears to confirm what she has been told.

She has also read Paul's rebuke to the quarrelsome Christians in Corinth who were told not to appeal to the court as a means for settling their disputes. To do so, Paul says, "is defeat for you." Instead, "suffer wrong," he commands (1 Corinthians 6:1-7, RSV).

And she has read Paul's instruction to wives that they be subject to their husbands "in everything" (Ephesians 5:22-24).

Melinda seems to have two options:

1. She can file civil charges against her husband and cease being a Christian, or

2. She can remain a Christian and continue to endure the sexual abuse that will endanger her physical and mental health, and may even lead to her death.

Melinda's problem may be a distasteful one, but the question it raises is often faced by Christians: What rights do Christians have? What are Christians to do when they have been defrauded, are the subjects of gross injustice, or are living under threat of violence? Do Christians have rights, or does being Christian mean that for Christ's sake we must suffer abuse without taking any action to halt it?

The Argument Against Christian Rights

Before we rush to answer these questions, let's look at why some thoughtful Christians believe Christ's disciples should not appeal to rights for protection.

Throughout the history of the church there have been leaders who have held that Christians should renounce all forms of self-defense—much less retaliation—including appeal to "rights" before the law. According to these leaders, Christians who seek to defend themselves after having been treated unfairly display a lack of faith in God and a glaring misconception of what it means to be a Christian. On the other hand, by refusing to defend their "rights," Christians demonstrate faith in God's care and protection; they thereby follow their Lord who went defenseless to the Cross, trusting only in His Father.

Christians who insist on defending their rights, the argument goes, place too much importance on this world and not enough on the world to come. They renounce their faith in God, contribute to the kingdom of selfishness and violence, and surrender their confidence that the kingdom of Christ will triumph over the kingdoms of this world.

This argument is not one that encourages Christians to patiently and passively endure evil. What it does encourage is faithful nonresistance to evil. Echoing the words of Jesus in the Sermon on the Mount, Paul in Romans 12:14-21 instructs the Roman Christians to "overcome evil with good" (v. 21). Fundamental to the Christian faith and ethic is a confidence that the most effective way to overcome evil in the world is not through more evil, but by doing good to those who are evil. When we meet violence with violence, whatever the form—verbal, psychological, physical—we breed more violence.

Christians have as their model the God who did not deal with us according to our sins, but who forgave us and drew us to himself. Those who, like their Lord, overcome evil by doing good possess a more powerful weapon than any sword, police force, or court. By responding as did their Lord, Christians present to the offender a higher vision of what life can be. To overcome evil with good is the only effective way to overcome evil and to bring about real reconciliation among adversaries. The question is not *Should* we resist evil? but *How* should we resist evil?

Problems with the Argument Against Christian Rights

While the argument against Christian rights is to be appreciated and must play a major role in any answer we might propose, we need to consider some important qualifications to the argument.

First, the same apostle who counseled the Corinthians to settle their disputes within the fellowship and who on numerous occasions endured abuse from his opponents, also asserted his rights as a Roman citizen on at least three occasions.

Having been falsely accused by his Jewish opponents, and having been bounced around in the Roman bureaucracy, Paul said in effect, "I am tired of the runaround and empty accusations. There is nothing to your charges, and I refuse to be victimized by them. I appeal to Caesar!" (see Acts 25:10-11). The Roman legal system allowed citizens facing capital charges to appeal to Caesar. On two other occasions Paul appealed to his rights as a Roman citizen, once when he halted preparations being made to scourge him (22:25), and previously when he and Silas were prisoners at Philippi (16:35-39).

If we may judge by Paul's actions, there are times when it is in keeping with the teaching of Jesus to appeal to the appropriate authorities for protection against injustice. The difficulty comes in trying to figure out when and in what form such appeals should occur.

For example, what should a Christian owner of an automobile dealership do when he discovers his business partner has cheated the company out of $2 million and has jeopardized both the future of the dealership and the livelihood of the Christian partner's family? Should he, because he is a Christian, refuse to prosecute the offender? If the answer is yes, then why did Paul appeal to Caesar?

Second, are there not instances in which Christians act immorally and unfaithfully if they refuse to employ force, even if force means a court injunction to halt the sale of pornographic literature or to insure due process to an accused person?

Should Christians in Germany in the 1930s have refused forcefully to oppose Hitler's rise to power? Would returning good for evil have stopped him? Should Christians not utilize the press, the courts, and legislatures to oppose social evil? And if they do not employ whatever force is necessary to prevent injustices and social chaos, do they not abandon the world to those who would seize it for their own evil purposes?

There are sharp disagreements among equally committed Christians over how these questions should be answered. With this in mind, is there an answer to the question we've raised about Christian rights? Or are Christians simply left to act in a twilight of uncertainty? Let's at least try to lay the basis for an answer.

An Answer to the Question

1. To begin with, I would agree with those who say Christians have no rights, neither in the church nor in the world. That is, Christians have no rights simply because they are Christians.

We are Christians purely by God's grace, and our place in the Kingdom is His gift, not the result of something that is rightfully ours. The church, as a part of the kingdom of God, is not an arena in which individuals should struggle for territorial ownership and defend their "rights." The Corinthian Christians did not understand this; tearing apart the Body of Christ, they insisted on their rights and fought one against another. The church betrays itself when it becomes a battleground for power struggles and competition between wills. People who understand that only by God's grace are we accepted should be the same people who realize that everything important for salvation is already secure. Therefore, to fight for "rights" in the church is to subvert the gospel.

Furthermore, neither do Christians—as Christians—have rights in the world. Followers of Christ have no legitimate claim to special social acceptance, prestige, political influence, or protection against abuse and exploitation. A person cannot legitimately say, "I am a Christian, and I have a right not to be persecuted for being a Christian." To identify fully with Christ involves becoming just as vulnerable as He was. "The call to Christian discipleship," said theologian Dietrich Bonhoeffer, "is a call to come and die." "The church," he said, "needs only so much space in the world as is necessary to bear faithful witness to Christ."

One of the historic errors of Christianity has been its frequent effort to marry itself to the state and its power in an attempt to escape vulnerability. "Wrap the church in the garments of civil authority," this deception has insisted, "surround the church with the powers of the state to force a Christian program on society, then Christianity will become invulnerable."

In democratic nations, Christians have no more rights than do Muslims, Buddhists, or Jews. This fact seems especially difficult for Christians in the United States to accept. But the fact remains: Christians have no rights.

2. But while Christians do not have rights, citizens do.

One of the main characteristics of democracies today is that the state exists by the will of the people. And the function of the state is to protect rights the people identify as unreleasable, inalienable.

Another primary feature of the democratic state is that one's rights are supposed to have nothing to do with religious, sexual, or political identity. This truth has been, and is still being, established with great difficulty. In the United States, for example, one can point to a history of legislation and landmark court decisions by which abstract rights have been made concretely secure.

Closely associated with rights and citizenship is justice, which makes it possible for a person to achieve the dignity that is his by right of citizenship and humanity. The state in which Melinda lives has a law against spousal rape because being forced to live merely to satisfy someone's sexual fantasies is a violation of human dignity; such actions are flagrantly unjust. To ignore Melinda's rights is to encourage injustice, not only against her, but against society. She has a right to be free from mistreatment, not primarily as a Christian, but as a citizen of a democratic society in which rights are secured by an enforceable constitution.

To a large extent, our democratic understanding of justice and rights comes from the biblical concern for justice, especially from the words of Jesus. According to philosopher Alfred North Whitehead, once the gospel's high estimate of people was set loose in the stream of Western history, all artificial standards that condone and institutionalize injustice were bound to collapse in time. The drive to abolish slavery, for example, received its moral force largely from the estimate of human worth established by Christ.

Although the Bible does not provide lists of "human rights," it does reveal that a thirst for justice is indispensable if we want to express our worship of and love for God. Rights embody God's will for His creation; He, not man, is the Provider and primary Protector of human rights.

Had the Bible provided a list of rights, it would have included the sanctity of life; the right not to be permanently deprived of land; equality in the means of livelihood, and where this is not possible, equality of opportunity; the right to rest from work one day in seven; the right of a servant of God not to be the servant of anyone else; the right to be protected from the arbitrary exercise of power; and equality before the law for all classes.[2]

What Should We Do Next?

Having explained a few of the diverse aspects of our difficult question, let us now try to develop an answer.

1. First, if to pursue justice is to recognize that creation belongs to God, that He loves all people, wants us to get along together, and has Kingly authority over us, then the defense of rights becomes a Christian responsibility.

It is part of our job assignment; it's not a questionable option. By pursuing justice, we claim this world as God's own. He is the Lord, not the powers of this age that promote and institutionalize injustice.

2. Second, the pursuit of justice is not mainly concerned with "getting what's due me."

Appeal to civil and legal rights by Christians for themselves and for others is in keeping with the gospel so long as it is not done for the purposes of retaliation or to expand conflict and alienation.

The Sermon on the Mount, in fact, clearly portrays the gospel's power (1) to break the unending cycles of hate and retaliation that develop between people and nations, and (2) to make reconciliation possible. The gospel of our Lord stands not against a concern for justice but against a desire for vengeance that intoxicates people and often captures entire societies.

3. Third, Christians ought to think of rights in terms of responsibility.

These include responsibility for the gospel, for the

church and civil community, and for finding ways to bring about a reconciliation. In many instances—in Melinda's case, for example—possibilities for reconciliation may be marginal. In situations like these, mere protection by the law may be all we can achieve. However, considering all limitations, when the Christian acts in a manner that is truly Christian, he will always be looking for ways to move beyond minimal justice and toward reconciliation and healing.

1. This name and some other details in the story have been changed.
2. Steven Mott, *Biblical Ethics and Social Change* (New York: Oxford University Press, 1982), 52.

Al Truesdale is professor of Christian ethics at Nazarene Theological Seminary, Kansas City.

OTHER DIALOG SERIES TITLES

A Christian Attitude Toward Attitudes

Christian Personality Under Construction

Christians at Work in a Hurting World

Clean Living in a Dirty World

Dear God, Help Me Understand

Growing Season: Maturing of a Christian

How to Improve Your Prayer Life

How to Live the Holy Life

I Believe: Now Tell Me Why

Less Stress, Please

The Me I See: A Christian Approach to Self-Esteem

Misguiding Lights?

No Easy Answers

Questions You Shouldn't Ask About Christianity

Questions You Shouldn't Ask About the Church

Raising Kids

Spiritual Zest

Turning Points

What Jesus Said About . . .

When Life Gets Rough

For a description of all available Dialog Series books, including some that may not be listed here, ask for a free brochure from your favorite Christian bookstore, your denominational distributor, or Beacon Hill Press of Kansas City.